SHOULD I GO BACK

WHY GIVING YOUR MARRIAGE ONE LAST TRY
COULD ACTUALLY HELP YOU MOVE ON

SHOULD I GO BACK

JANEEN GOLIGHTLY

LitPrime
"Your story is our priority"

LitPrime Solutions
21250 Hawthorne Blvd
Suite 500, Torrance, CA 90503
www.litprime.com
Phone: 1-800-981-9893

© 2023 Janeen Golightly. All rights reserved.

No part of this book may be reproduced, stored in a retrieval system, or transmitted by any means without the written permission of the author.

Published by LitPrime Solutions   10/20/2023

ISBN: 979-8-88703-224-5(sc)
ISBN: 979-8-88703-225-2(hc)
ISBN: 979-8-88703-226-9(e)

Library of Congress Control Number: 2023907273

Any people depicted in stock imagery provided by iStock are models, and such images are being used for illustrative purposes only.

Certain stock imagery © iStock.

Because of the dynamic nature of the Internet, any web addresses or links contained in this book may have changed since publication and may no longer be valid. The views expressed in this work are solely those of the author and do not necessarily reflect the views of the publisher, and the publisher hereby disclaims any responsibility for them.

For my children, Dirk, Tia, and Gabby. Without you in my life, I would certainly be less happy, less motivated, and not nearly as strong as I have become. The challenges I faced while raising the three of you were an adventure for all of us. Thank you for the laughter and the love. I am grateful I get to be your mom.

Because of each of you, I have grown to be a better person in so many ways. And I thank you all for that.

CONTENTS

INTRODUCTION		IX
1	MY STORY	1
2	WHY GIVING YOUR MARRIAGE ONE LAST TRY COULD ACTUALLY HELP YOU MOVE ON	13
3	DIVORCE MEANS CHANGES AND MORE CHANGES	97
4	LIVING WITH MULTIPLE MARRIAGES AND DIVORCES	105
5	SELF-IMPROVEMENT	111
6	WHAT ABOUT YOUR EMOTIONAL HEALTH?	122
7	BEGIN TO IMPROVE IN THIRTY (30 DAYS, 30 WEEKS – PICK YOUR OWN TIMEFRAME)	134
8	CAN YOU BE HAPPY IN A DIFFICULT MARRIAGE?	150

9	THIRTY WAYS TO LOVE YOUR HUSBAND	156
10	THIRTY WAYS TO LOVE YOUR WIFE	160
11	HOW DO I FIND THE RIGHT PERSON TO MARRY IN THE FIRST PLACE?	181
12	CREATE YOUR PERFECT SPOUSE	185
13	INDULGE ME, HONEY	190
14	TEN REASONS TO KEEP IT TOGETHER	195
15	SHOULD I GO BACK	202
16	THE ENDING TO MY STORY – AT LEAST FOR NOW	206
17	A FEW FINAL WORDS – FROM A FRIEND	213

ACKNOWLEDGMENTS ... 217

ABOUT THE AUTHOR ... 221

INTRODUCTION

The idea for *Should I Go Back: Why Giving Your Marriage One Last Try Could Actually Help You Move On* came from my desire over the years to share my experiences of marriage and divorce with others who might be going through similar things. For a very long time, I have thought about ways I could speak to you, help you, and let you know you are certainly not alone.

Not only are you not alone, you are also not so different in your experiences or in your ways of dealing with a difficult marriage. There are a lot of marriage counselors and therapists out there who can help guide us to better marriages and ways of dealing with difficult spouses. They can give us the tools to work on our relationships, and they can tell us that divorce will not solve the long-term problem. But until you have actually lived it, you will never truly understand that divorce is not always a solution—it is simply, in a lot of cases, a change.

That said, I have learned about and personally experienced the complete and utter assurance that comes over you when you know there is no future in your current situation. When you reach that end – there is really no turning back. The only way out is forward. And that means divorce is inevitable. This book is meant to be a guide to understanding your own very personal experiences and where they are ultimately taking you. Whether you decide to work things out or move ahead with divorce, you will know you did everything you could to salvage the relationship. And that, my friends, is exactly where you want to be. That is the secret to moving on to becoming a happy, healthy and whole person.

If you're reading this book, you're likely considering getting divorce for the very first time. I am going to be extremely honest about the realities of divorce. You may not like some of the things I'm going to tell you, but please consider the things you read here and take a deep look into your own situation. I'm not trying to change your mind about following through with divorce if it's the best thing for you and your family. But please take to heart my suggestions for making a difficult situation the best it can be.

Divorce is, most definitely, an escape - at first. And then it becomes the road to new, and possibly more heart-breaking problems. But it also just might be the road to a new, joyful relationship with a wonderful person who fills your world with love. How can that happen? By bringing two healthy individuals together who have freed themselves from guilt after leaving a bad situation, but done so while keeping relationships intact – never easy! How do I know this to be true? Because I have done it both ways.

Divorce has become so accepted. It used to be that you were the odd one out if you had divorced parents. But that simply isn't true anymore. Our kids are quickly becoming victims of the cycle we have created. And what will they think about marriage when they grow up and want to have families of their own?

This book is an attempt to help you learn, through my experiences, that taking charge of the things you can control will, in many cases, save your marriage. And if it can't save your marriage, at least it can save your family and each person in it. But you have to be open-minded. You have to find the humility. And you have to be willing.

I believe, at this point in my life, that working on myself and my own shortcomings and issues could have possibly saved my first marriage in the very beginning. If I could have done that, I would have saved myself and my kids a lot of pain and chaos over the past several years. But that's me and my story. That may not be you or your story. There are a lot of reasons people can't make a marriage work. But I believe that selfishness comes into play at some point from one spouse or the other.

That said - I do think that sometimes two good people share an attraction, come together, and for one reason or another they begin to bring out the worst in each other. And they find it necessary to part ways and find other people who they are more compatible with. Truth be told – both individuals most likely knew during the dating period that they weren't a good match, but sometimes we just don't want to admit that we don't belong together – most likely because we don't want to give up the physical aspect of the relationship. Marriage is a lifelong, even eternal commitment, so it is a good idea to think long-term and determine if you see yourself having a family, working through problems, and growing old together BEFORE you marry. But, if you're reading this book, it's probably too late for that!

I had a friend tell me once that you can be in love with someone – from a distance. You can have feelings for them, but still know they are not the person you should marry. That was one of the wisest pieces of advice I had ever received in my life, and I can gratefully say that this one solid piece of advice has saved me recently. I look at potential relationships a lot differently now. Of course, we want romantic love. But there must also be a lot of other things that fall into place too. We need compatibility in a lot of areas – religion, politics, kids, lifestyle, backgrounds, fitness levels, food choices, similar recreational interests – the more commonality we can find, the more wonderful our relationships will be.

The thing is, the pain and chaos of divorce never fully go away. Yes, they fade over time, and yes, the experiences gained are invaluable. But the long-term effects of divorce can be far-reaching, and they can remain for a lifetime. In my case, I learned the hard way that a couple of my kids would feel the effects of a broken home well into adulthood. I don't know for certainty that the divorce was necessarily to blame in and of itself – but perhaps the decisions that followed my first divorce.

As you read this book, try to put your own life in perspective. Think about each of your children and how you believe they may react to their parents getting a divorce. Try and put yourself in their shoes, and imagine what they will go through when their dad moves out of the house, or you pick them up and move in with your own parents. Think about their emotional state, and try to put your own issues aside. If divorce needs to happen – accept that. And then be methodical about what you do next and how you and your soon-to-be ex-spouse handle things. This is where being a mature and thoughtful person becomes necessary.

Whether your kids are just young, teenagers, or young adults – even married adults, getting through divorce with everyone's healthy mindset intact is the goal. And I like to believe it can be done. I have seen it happen.

I know how easy it can be to minimize or even forget about the kids' personal struggles and experiences because we can become so self-absorbed when our marriage is failing. If we can focus on our kids' wellbeing, I think we can make better decisions in every way.

The biggest reason I'm writing this book is because I know all this! I have lived all this! And I wish I could have seen these words staring at me when I was seriously considering divorce for the very first time.

But I also know that if you've reached that point where divorce is simply the only option:

You will be okay.

Your kids will be okay.

There is life after divorce, and it can be joyful!

But be smart. This book is meant to help you do just that, whether you end up staying in your marriage or deciding to start over.

For those of you who are stuck – who may have already left a marriage that simply was not working, but can't seem to pull the trigger on finalizing that divorce… I have devoted a chapter to you. Look closely at the title of this book, *Should I Go Back: Why Giving Your Marriage One Last Try Could Actually Help You Move On*.

I have a dear friend who has suffered through this scenario for a few years – not living with his spouse, but also not divorced. Wanting to move forward, but not being able to. No one can reason with a person who is stuck. They have to find their own way. They are most likely stuck because they feel guilt, moral judgment, fear of the unknown, preconceived notions about the financial burdens they think they may experience, or any number of negative feelings that may be keeping them from moving toward a more fulfilling new life.

So - read on, and promise yourself right now that you will do the things outlined in this book.

Give yourself the best shot at keeping your marriage intact.

And if that turns out not to be an option for you, then give yourself the best shot at being the healthiest version of yourself you can possibly be so you will have wonderful things to offer to your kids, to your future spouse, and most importantly – to yourself. And even more importantly, give your kids the best shot at having two healthy parents who will be happy, solid, supportive examples who can get along with each other and move on to loving relationships with people who can accept your children, be involved in their lives, and give everyone the ability to be who they are without judgment or pressure. These are things that can be hard to find in a second marriage. But if you can be strong and committed to your expectations, I believe you can attract someone into your life who can offer these things.

I have many friends in second marriages who have found compatible partners who love their kids and respect the fact that they had a life before them. I love to see divorced people come together and give each other the freedom to be who they have become - and have the strength to combine their lives together while still respecting the fact that they both had a full life already. Two healthy and whole individuals coming together to enhance what each other already has.

I remember having a conversation with my close friend whose marriage ended around the same time as my last marriage ended. He remarried shortly after his divorce, and we ran into each other one night. After telling me about the trials he'd been experiencing, he made a comment that he wished his new wife would understand that he just wanted to celebrate his kids' birthdays and other important events with his kids alone. In a second marriage, why couldn't that be a thing? I'm going to be honest and say that I agreed with him. I think we have to be open to unusual ways of doing things when we blend families. Their situation is a difficult one, and my friend wants so badly to keep his relationship with his kids intact. It's been a struggle for all of them in many ways. These are some of the very real issues that can arise. It's trying to keep that balance of developing a solid relationship with your new spouse, and keeping a healthy relationship with your children. Not an easy task.

Some of you may already be on your second or third marriage and you're looking for help because you simply don't want to get divorced again. Not everything in this book will apply to your situation, but it's up to you to find the things in these pages that will help you find your answer and your happiness. I think a good place to start is by writing down what the positives are. Ask yourself if your spouse provides a sense of security. Ask yourself if your spouse good to your kids. Ask yourself if you have a good life. Start with these things and go from there.

Good luck.

And remember you have the power to change not only your circumstances, but yourself.

CHAPTER ONE

MY STORY

My kids threaten me all the time that my obituary, when I die, will read as follows…

Janeen Kaye Severson Rider Golightly Diamond.

Yes, they like to make light of the fact that I have been married three times—and divorced three times. But if we didn't spend time laughing about it, we'd probably all be more messed up over it than we already are. A healthy sense of humor, in my opinion, is the key to success in every aspect of life!

So, this is my story. And by the end of it, I hope you will come to realize that living a happy, healthy, vibrant life, whether as a partner in a successful marriage or alone after a divorce, isn't about luck. It's entirely up to you and the choices you make!

It all started when I was seventeen years old. I met the "man of my dreams" and fell instantly in love. It didn't hurt that his best friend was dating my best friend, which made for some really fun times. And it didn't even dawn on me when we went rabbit hunting and actually ate our catch for dinner that this wasn't really going to be the man who could give me the life I had always dreamed of. After all, my best friend was right there with me, and it was really just an extension of our friendship. It all felt good, and getting married was what I had thought about for most of my high school years. I couldn't wait to get started on being an adult and living my own life. Marriage was the fastest way, I thought at the time, to achieve this.

My first husband and I married just shy of my nineteenth birthday. I was blissfully happy —the wedding, the dress, the gifts, the cake, all of our friends showing up to wish us well and telling me how beautiful I looked. We lived in a small town, and it was a huge celebration. It truly was an amazing wedding.

I felt happy during that first year of marriage—when we moved into our first apartment, when I cooked my first dinner, when our best friends moved in next door. That first year was full of a lot of good times—but I also felt like I was drowning. I was not mature enough to handle even the slightest criticism or the immature remarks that hurt my feelings. And my husband was not mature enough to make me feel like he had married the most beautiful woman in the world. I think I truly expected marriage to hold a nonstop, endless supply of fun and intimacy. Everything was supposed to be about me, and I wanted my husband to see it that way too. And when it wasn't, well, there were plenty of "men" in the workplace who were willing to fill in where he was lacking.

We were KIDS and the immaturity was overflowing! And all that male attention coming my direction made me realize that I had so many more options out there. Why had I settled? What was I thinking? Six years and two kids later, I asked my husband for a divorce.

Now here's the part I want you to really pay attention to. I knew I would get to keep the house and any belongings I wanted. I knew I could take the best car. I knew the kids would be with me most of the time; except, of course, every other weekend. I knew my parents would pick up the slack and help me out with the kids when I was working or taking classes. I had a pretty good job and could afford my life, and I knew my ex-husband would be required to pay some kind of child support. So, I knew my life was going to be just fine without him.

How lucky could I possibly be?

Well, all these years later, I realize that what I should have been asking was, how selfish could I possibly be?

Almost everyone who knew me tried to talk me out of it. A couple of people even ditched me as a friend, but I knew that this was what I wanted! My kids were going to be fine—I mean, come on, they were only three and a half years, and three months old. Yep, that's what I said. I had a three-month-old baby girl! They would never even remember a time living with their dad, so we were good!

I can write about myself like this now because I am not this person any more. I'm being a little harsh on myself partly in good humor, but these words are not really all that far from the truth. Yes, my ex-husband played a big role in our getting a divorce. But I believe now that I had the power to make things better. I know now that I could have changed the dynamic between us – had I understood with my full heart and soul just how important the commitment of marriage is between two people.

I didn't leave my marriage because it was terrible. It certainly wasn't perfect. We had our problems like everyone does. But ultimately, I left because I, in my own mind, believed I could do better. And, in all fairness, my first husband was a really great person. And, also to be fair, I do believe had I stayed in this marriage we would have eventually divorced. We were not good together. We were very different in so many ways, and I can't imagine being with him now. I believe our big mistake was marrying so young, before we knew who we really were or what we wanted.

The details of the rest of my story don't matter much, but they do offer some entertainment value, so here goes.

A few weeks before my divorce was final, I met "the love of my life." We dated long-distance for one year. Now let me just say right here and now that long-distance dating, in my experience, is not a good idea. Oh, it feels really good! Every two weeks, after much anticipation, we'd get together after that lengthy separation, and it was kind of like going on a bunch of first dates. He'd call me every night and make me feel like he couldn't live without me. He was everything he wanted me to see—and more. But then, when I wanted him to marry me, he stopped calling, he stopped coming to see me, he began seeing someone else. I was devastated!

Luckily for me, Prince Charming was waiting in the wings to whisk me up and solve all my problems. He distracted me for a while, but ultimately, I was not happy with him and we broke up. The truth is, I wasn't happy with myself.

This time, I decided I was going to be smart at playing this game. I began a pattern of serial dating: Meet a guy, date for three months, break up. Meet another guy, date for three months, break up. Three months is that point where a guy either wants to take your relationship to the next level or move on. So, I wouldn't even give him a chance. Three months - done!

This went on for quite some time and then one day, I ran into someone I had known casually for a few years and learned that he too was now divorced. He wanted to date me. Now usually when your gut tells you this is a bad idea, you listen, right? Well, after a little consideration, I concluded that I'd just dabble a bit and run later. Two and a half years later, we were married.

He had some very wounded teenage daughters, an ex-wife who remarried and moved to another state shortly after we were married, no money and no house.

Just one month after we married, he lost his job. Now I was okay with all this because he had such a positive attitude, so I knew we could make this work. After all, I had a house, I had a job, and I had a young son and daughter whom he seemed to adore.

The details of this marriage are a riot but honestly, that's an entirely different book. Let me just say this - I could not love or accept his kids. His kids could not accept me. His ex-wife and I did not like each other. My kids could not accept him. He did not grow to love my kids. And we were at opposite ends of the spectrum as far as life was concerned. We could not agree on much. He could not stop spending money. And I grew very, very tired. I felt it was "better" for my two older kids that I ended that marriage.

But what about our daughter?

She was two when I divorced my husband after eight years of marriage!

And here we go again.

It was in this divorce where I truly experienced some hard knocks. I left at a time when I had no regular income, with a small child, and two teenagers to take care of. And yet, I had to go. I had reached that point where I just couldn't deal with the whole mess any more.

I knew I could go back into the workplace and find a job to support myself, and I knew I would do whatever it took to succeed.

I am a strong person, so I knew I could figure it out no matter what. After all, what's the worst that could happen, right?

Well let's see:

- Maybe he won't consistently pay child support.
- Maybe he'll take out bankruptcy instead of paying my settlement.
- Maybe he'll grow distant from our daughter because of his new life.
- Or maybe all of the above!

I was building a new home and waiting to move in, when two weeks before my closing date, I was informed that there would be no settlement. This meant I had no down payment for closing, and my payments would drastically increase now, leaving me with a whole lot of pressure that I didn't need.

The kids and I moved into our new home in December, two weeks before Christmas. I had borrowed the down-payment from my parents and managed to close on the house. But to be honest, I was scared. The kids each got a new pillow for Christmas—nothing more—and I told them we were going to have a nice dinner and sit around and talk about how grateful and blessed we were that we were able to move into our new home. That was all we were going to get that year for Christmas. They were great about it. It's one of those things we talk about even now. And when I tell that story, I cry. Not because it makes me sad, but because it was one of those experiences that brought us closer together as a family, and I am grateful for those memories at this point in my life.

But this was just the beginning.

The next two years were the most difficult and yet, most memorable time in my life. At least up to that point. I had landed a job with a marketing agency out of the blue, and, gratefully, I was getting enough freelance work every month to make ends meet. It was actually an incredible thing. I knew without a doubt that someone was watching out for me.

I made my bills every month, even though I rarely had anything left over after that. It was an experience that forced me to pull up my boot straps and keep moving forward. I literally stopped spending money. I paid for the house, the car, the heat, the lights, and the groceries. Anything else was considered a luxury, and we simply did without for as long as we had to. I hung on to the house for two years, until I had built up enough equity to sell it, pay my parents back, and put a decent amount into savings. I knew I had become stronger and more self-reliant. I could handle anything now.

This was one of those life-changing experiences that made me a better person.

Maybe not a smarter person yet, but definitely a better person.

Enter -- the "actual" love of my life. This story is difficult for me to tell, but worth a page or two because right at this point, I was walking in to the most heart wrenching experience I would ever have in my life -- and I had no idea.

In order to tell the full story – I have to backtrack just a little. A few months after my first divorce, before I married my second husband, I was introduced to a guy – remember the long-distance relationship I mentioned a couple of pages back? He was not at all someone I would have normally been interested in. We were different in almost every way two people can be different. And my gut was telling me right from the first day that getting involved with him was not a good idea. But… I wanted an adventure, and I decided to ignore my gut – just this once. He was not a particularly good-looking guy, so at first glance – easy to resist. But he was extremely charming and fun, and as much as I hate to admit it now, he reeled me in – hook, line and sinker!

Fast forward one year. We had been dating long distance, spending time with each other every couple of weeks, until one day – he simply disappeared. No warning, no explanation. Just gone! I was devastated! How can a person do that to another person? I thought he loved me.

Let me say here that I'm big on getting closure when a relationship ends. When you decide to leave someone, you owe them an explanation. One of the cruelest things you can do to a person is disappear. When someone you loved doesn't have closure, they can't move on – not really. I was forced to leave that relationship behind and move forward with my life, but I spent a painful year. About six months after he left, I received two dozen red roses at my office on my birthday! What? And then – a phone call! He was coming back! I was giddy – and then I was scared.

You know - the gut thing…

He said he was coming over that night, so I went

home, got dressed up and waited. And then I waited some more. Finally, around 1:00 in the morning – I went to bed and cried. That was the last time I ever heard from him, and I finally remarried about four years later.

I wish I could say this was the end of it!

But you know what I'm about to say.

After my second divorce, I was talking to a girlfriend one day and mentioned his name. She asked me if I was going to talk about him for the rest of my life! And then she told me I should call him. And I thought, you know – I guess I could. It had been 15 years since I'd last seen him. I had no idea if he was married or what his situation was at that point. But I needed to sit in front of him and get an explanation about what had happened. So, I emailed him, fully intending to meet with him and have a grown-up conversation about what happened that led to him walking away. I wanted closure.

Long story short – we were married 18 months later. I know!

Before I married him, I remember driving one day and thinking – I know this is wrong! But I didn't care. I just had to be with this guy. His charm had a hold on me and I was willing to risk everything! I was going to marry him. I didn't care what anyone else thought. My parents were sick about it, but they decided to lend their full support to my decision. My parents were extremely supportive, wonderful, amazing people. But I knew how they truly felt, and I wish that I had paid attention.

Our marriage was rocky to say the least. We had some really great times and we built a really wonderful life in so many ways. But he also made sure that everything was on his terms. I couldn't put my finger on why – but my feelings were hurt A LOT. He made me feel unimportant. I had already quit my job, and he wanted me to quit everything I was doing – my freelance work, my church work. He wanted me to be 100 percent dependent on him. I understood later on that he wanted to make sure I could never leave him.

I am proud to say that I did not quit everything I was doing. In the pit of my stomach I knew. I just wasn't sure exactly what it was that I knew. Until one day, after eight years of marriage, I got a phone call.

My oldest daughter called to ask if I was home. She was calling me from my front porch and said, "We need to talk, Mom." My heart sank. She had received a call from a woman that morning who told her she had a friend who had been sleeping with a married man for the past 11 years… And that man was my husband.

His relationship with this woman had been going on well before he and I started dating – and he NEVER LEFT HER!

Looking back, it's so easy to see that our story would end the way it did. There were so many red flags, and I chose to ignore them.

All this said, I strongly believe that our lives are meant to take certain directions to help us grow and help us learn important lessons. This is why I do not believe in regret. I don't believe in beating ourselves up over mistakes or misguided decisions. Ultimately, we become the people we are meant to be because of these experiences, or maybe even in spite of them. I am who I am today because of all my experiences. And I like who I am today.

My Mom used to ask me how I could stay so positive after going through so much turmoil in my relationships, and I would always say, "Mom, this is just a temporary setback." That was my mantra. That was my way of dealing with things and looking toward the future with hope and with excitement for new possibilities.

Here's the good news. I've been single now for the past eight plus years. I have finally taken the time to heal, the time to get my last daughter raised and just about graduated from college. I have a fantastic job and have recovered financially to a degree I could not have imagined ten years ago. My two oldest kids are married. And the time I've been able to have, alone, with my youngest daughter has been the most amazing time in my life. She and I are very close. We have been there for each other. And she has grown to be a beautiful, healthy, wonderful young woman.

I love my life, and I love where I am. And I'm not in a hurry to jump back into another relationship. Truthfully, I have always loved my life – even with all of the changes I have gone through. I don't believe divorce defines a person, and I also don't believe a relationship is always needed for a person to be happy.

Would I prefer being in a relationship? Yes. But waiting for the right one means happiness and joy in the long run.

CHAPTER TWO

WHY GIVING YOUR MARRIAGE ONE LAST TRY COULD ACTUALLY HELP YOU MOVE ON

I believe, with some hard work and a lot of desire, we can begin to make changes in ourselves and in our marriages almost immediately. For me, this realization came after a lot of mistakes, a lot of experience, and a lot of pain. When I look back over my story, my telling of it is meant to be humorous, but the living of it was extremely difficult – not just for me, but for everyone involved.

The men I married were good men in their own right. The problems weren't all because of them, but rather because of us. I learned over the years that relationships can't work if you - the person who is responsible for yourself and your behavior - won't look outside yourself. When two people enter a marriage, I see clearly now that they should enter it with a plan to care for each other, serve each other, and do everything in their power to show love and affection, and true commitment. If two people who have that attitude get married – I believe their chances of a successful marriage almost have to increase significantly.

By the time two people are planning to divorce they have most likely already reached what they believe to be that point of no return. And that may be true. But based on my own experiences, I'm convinced that going in for one last try – with your whole heart – is absolutely necessary, and here's why:

- It's possible you and your spouse could find some common ground during that one last attempt that will bring you back together. Depending on the cause - sometimes people actually can forgive each other and begin again. Just maybe – focusing on the marriage and on each other for a solid month, can begin to make a difference. Just maybe going in for one last try will help you fall back in love. I can tell you that often after the divorce is done, that's the time some people begin to realize they really did love each other, and there really were a lot of good things about their marriage. It can take getting divorced to see clearly. So maybe it's worth trying to get that clarity BEFORE a divorce. I say it's worth a shot.

- I am not in agreement with people staying together in a bad situation simply for the sake of not getting divorced. Sadly, I think we all know people like this – those who stay because they believe they are taking the moral high ground, and in the meantime, everyone involved suffers quietly. Which brings me to my second point…

Going back for one last try could help you be happier in the long run once you do finally get divorced. I remember one night right before filing for my last divorce - I had a bit of a meltdown. I had already been divorced twice and just didn't want to face the thought of doing it again. I wondered if it would be possible for me to just forgive all the wrongs and literally start over in the marriage. I wanted so badly to just pretend like none of the trauma had ever happened. I wondered if it could be possible for me to just erase the past. My husband was desperate for me to do so. And so - I did. I went back in for one last try. For five months, life was amazing. It was better than it had been our entire marriage. He worked hard to show me just how much I meant to him. We went on a couple of trips and turned up the romance like never before. I began to believe it just might be possible for us to actually come back together. We were putting our full energy into making this marriage work and, for a time, I thought we were going to make it. Proof that if two people want it bad enough – it is entirely possible.

And then, one night, I came around the corner and walked into our closet – just in time to see him hiding his phone in the clothes on the top shelf. My heart sank. Sadly, this was the blessing in disguise. I had done everything in my power to save that marriage, and I knew it. When I finally asked him to leave, I was completely at peace. I knew I had to let the marriage go at that moment, and I was ready.

To all of you who are "stuck" in a place of limbo... I think the reason people get stuck is because of what I just described. Their situations and reasons might be different, but they may be holding onto a scenario that isn't real or even possible. They can't see what is really going on, and I think some good people hold onto a marriage way too long for fear of disappointing people, or for fear of making the wrong decision, or because they have misconceptions about what divorce will look like financially for them. Fear holds people back sometimes, but get out there and live your life! Find your happiness, whether it's with your current spouse, with a new love, or alone. Life is just too short! When you know in your heart it's over – move on and get back to living a happy life!

I was willing to forgive my husband for everything he had done, but he was not willing to change his behavior. That scenario is never going to work. I needed to see it firsthand and in living color before I could fully let go. Going back for one last try, after you've stepped back for a while, can help you see with your eyes fully open exactly what is really going on in the marriage, and you will likely remember why you left in the first place. For me, everything came clear in that moment, and I have never looked back.

So, let's take some action! I'm talking to all of you – those who want to try and save their marriages, those who want to find the way to peacefully move on, and those who find themselves stuck between separation and divorce. This exercise can help you begin to see clearly.

The following pages contain an exercise that I've divided into 30 days for the purpose of mindfully focusing on each other and on your marriage for one month. My passion for writing this book came from realizing that once you leave your original marriage – especially if children are involved – life is just never going to be the same. I'm not at all saying it won't be good, or even so much better. I'm simply saying it will bring some challenges you cannot begin to fathom until you have gone through these things.

Keep in mind, I'm not a marriage counselor or a therapist. This exercise is simply a list of the things I wish I would have done before deciding to leave my FIRST marriage. They are things I wish I would have given some serious consideration to and thoughtfully tried before making such a major, life-changing decision. Second and third marriages can be easier to leave, and that is part of the reason I feel so strongly about being certain that leaving that original marriage is what you want or need to do.

So, let's take a look at the thirty days.

And let me say here, even though you have full access to the entire thirty-day exercise, these are meant to be completed one day at a time. I feel like you need a full thirty days to clear your head and work through things. Sure, you can do multiple assignments on one day, but rushing through this exercise is not the intention. I want you to take it slowly and give your full attention to just one idea per day. Most of these exercises aren't going to take you all day to complete – but the idea is to give each one your full consideration for the entire day. And, if you need a few days between exercises, take them. If it takes three months to complete the full thirty days, fine! Just make it to the end.

Let's get started.

DAY 1

Break Off Any Affairs

The next thirty days are going to be thought provoking, challenging, and some days, downright hard! But if you'll trust yourself, you can come out the other side in a better place—I promise you that. You may save your marriage. And if not, well, you'll know you've given it everything you had. And whatever decision you come to will be the right one for you.

This very first assignment, for some of you, is going to be the hardest. But you must do it if you're going to move forward and give this a shot. So here goes. If someone else is in the picture, you have to commit right now to breaking it off for the next thirty days. Ideally, you will break it off permanently because you will determine that you ARE going to work on your marriage going forward. That means no contact—no calling, no texting, no Facebooking, nothing (no kidding) — while you go through this exercise.

Unfortunately, a lot of divorces happen because of affairs. If there are or were affairs, you should think seriously about getting out of your marriage. But now let me qualify that statement: if there are affairs that the person refuses to end. I happen to know people whose marriages have survived affairs. But it takes a major commitment, huge amounts of forgiveness, and lots of changes to make a marriage work once it has been violated like that. In order to gain someone's trust back, you are both going to have to be patient. I think it a whole lot harder to RE-gain someone's trust than to gain it in the first place.

And did I mention it's going to take a lot of work! So that's your assignment today.

Just a Sidenote.

There are many different reasons why people have affairs.

In my experience,

- one of you may not be getting what you need emotionally from the marriage, so you step outside;
- one of you might simply need or want an excuse to end the marriage, because, after all, it's hard for the other to argue with infidelity;
- some people are just cheaters who like to live on the edge, in which case, it's time to end the marriage;
- or it could be a cry for help – meaning, there is something wrong in the marriage and one of you may see this as the only way to grab the other's attention.

These are all very real possibilities. If an affair is happening in your marriage, you will both have to decide if it can be dealt with. And then you will have to conclude whether or not the marriage can survive. I can only speak from personal experience – but this type of betrayal is extremely hard to forgive and nearly impossible to live with.

I have seen women say they can forgive their husband's affair and stay in the marriage. I think most women will live with a lot of things before giving up because they just don't want to be divorced. But ultimately, an affair is not an easy thing to forgive and, in my experience, the resentment settles back in over time. Or if their husband or wife was cheating, he or she may not be able to give it up and will cheat again.

Some couples can come back together and truly forgive and forget – but it takes A LOT of work and a lot of effort. I definitely believe it's worth a try for the reasons mentioned in this book:

- It's possible you may just be able to truly come back together,
- It will give you the absolute knowledge that you either can or cannot stay in the marriage,
- It will give you the closure you need if you decide to leave for good.

Keep in mind that you can love someone and not have to be married to them. Just because we love a person does not mean we are required to be in a long-term relationship with them. We need to be mature enough to realize that feelings and compatibility just sometimes don't mesh. If a person is ultimately not a fit for us, not loyal, not faithful, not as excited as we are to be in a relationship, or just plain not good for us – it's okay to move along. I have learned that once you get yourself in a healthy relationship, the memories of your past relationships become just that – memories. And it's wonderful to have memories of good times, but it doesn't have to be everything.

I saw something recently that pointed out how when we keep thinking about a person from our past and we keep hurting – we tend to believe it's because we are still in love with that person. But actually, what we are feeling is PTSD from all of the pain that relationship caused us. This hit me like a ton of bricks.

Affairs, complicated past relationships and painful breakups can affect us all – but putting them into perspective and learning from a knowledgeable therapist what is really going on can make all the difference in the world. It's going to mean that you will be able to move on to a healthy relationship and leave the past behind.

Wouldn't life be so much easier if we knew and understood ourselves from the very beginning, if we knew what and who we wanted and those things were reciprocated by the other person? We can cause ourselves a lot of pain by holding on to our love for another person – even when that love isn't returned. It's easy to ask ourselves – why would we want to be with someone who doesn't love us back? But until we can sort through the root of those feelings and figure ourselves out, we will continue to feel pain and may even stay in relationships that we have no business being in.

Not all therapists are created equal. Some are better than others, and if you can find someone who can help you see past your "feelings" – I believe you're in the right place. That's my humble opinion in watching myself, friends, kids and people I love experience therapy and progress to a better place.

DAY 2

List the Positives in Your Marriage

I'm glad to see you back here today. That means you either didn't have to do yesterday's assignment, or you took care of it and want to seriously give your marriage another chance. Good for you! Please be completely honest with yourself. Pretending it's not a thing when it really is – is like going to a therapist and asking for help without telling them the truth about what's really going on in your life. What's the point?

Let me just say again, this exercise is meant to be completed over a period of at least thirty days—one assignment per day, or longer if you need more time. Some of you may have taken a week or even a month to take care of Day 1 – it doesn't matter how long it takes to make progress. The point is that you are moving forward and really focusing on the things that are going to matter in the long run. So, don't try to rush through it and do several things each day. You need at least thirty days to clear your head and focus. This is not something to be brushed over if you're serious about it. And I want you to spend each day focusing on just one thing, even if it's an easy assignment that day. If it takes 30 days just to end an affair and know in the deepest part of your heart and sould that you're not going back – then take 30 days!

Today, I want you to sit down somewhere quiet and

peaceful—and make a list of all the positive things you remember about your marriage. That's it. Take time to reflect on all of the good memories, the difficult times that brought you closer together, the trips, the conversations, the events in your marriage that made life so wonderful, the intimate moments, the hard work you did to accomplish things together, your first house, the things you created together, the support you gave each other - you get the idea. And once you have your list, I want you to go over it several times today and try to think back on all the good times you've had as a couple, and also that you've had as a family.

Sound easy enough? Then get on it.

Just a Sidenote.

Every marriage has good and bad. The goal is to try and have more of the good—most of the time. If you are both reasonable people, this should be attainable. Sometimes we feel we are reasonable but the other person is not. The frustrating reality is that we only have control over our own level of reason. Part of what I hope you will learn as you read this book, is that you can't fight what the other person in your marriage chooses to do or not do.

There is nothing more liberating than reaching that point where you either 1) let go of the control and accept the reality and know you can live with it, or 2) reach the point of being able to accept what is and walk away from it – and never look back.

I think there are some key points that can help us let go of the control. Ideally, both spouses can do this, but only focus on what you can do:

- Meet in the middle by compromising.
- Be willing to let each other be who he or she is without trying to change them.
- Remember, you are in control of your own happiness. Instead of controlling your spouse, do what makes you happy. For example, my husband went out of town on "business" a lot. Over time, I discovered that instead of getting upset about it, I could use that time as an opportunity to do the things I needed to do and wanted to do. And that is exactly what I did.

DAY 3

List the Ways Divorce Will Change Your Life

I hope you came up with a good list yesterday of all the positive things you remember about your marriage. Today, we're going to make another list. This time, I want you to go back to your favorite quiet and peaceful spot and make a list of all the ways divorce is going to change your life. Now this can be both good and bad; you may want to make two separate lists for this exercise.

- If the good outweighs the bad – you may start to realize your marriage is actually worth trying to hang on to.
- If the bad outweighs the good, you may have some things to work through or you may be closer to your decision to divorce.

Oftentimes, we jump into a divorce thinking "I can't wait to get away from this" or "I will be so happy to be done with that"—without really taking the time to think through all of the ramifications. For instance,

- You may forget you are going to have to move out of a neighborhood you love,
- or deal with the kids giving up their friends.
- Divorce isn't just about giving up your spouse—it's about giving up the life you currently have.

- It's about your kids having to change their lives and routines.
- Remember that!

So, get to your favorite spot and start working on your list.

Just a Sidenote.

If you like change and look upon it as a new adventure, I think that's healthy! But keep in mind that your kids may not share your view. I've been through so many changes in my life, it's amazing I'm still sane! But it's even more amazing that my kids have come through this whole thing alive and well. Keep their well-being in mind as you decide to make changes that will affect them.

DAY 4

List How Your Kids Will Be Negatively Affected

By today, you should have two well-thought-out lists – the first one listing out all the positive things about your marriage, and the second, a list of all the ways your life will change after divorce. And you should have spent some time pondering them. So now that you're into the list-making mode, we're going to make one last list before moving on with some more difficult assignments.

Today's list is going to focus on your kids. If you don't have kids, spend today going back over and adding to your lists from the previous two days. But if you do have kids—even if they are grown—do this assignment.

Make a list of how your kids will be negatively affected.

Because my kids were so small, this is something I gave almost no thought to at all! I kept telling myself that they're so young they won't even remember, and they won't know anything different.

What about realizing right now that your kids are going to grow up without their dad in the home, and that is no small thing. It will come back to them at some point. Life is just not that simple.

So, get to work on your list, and be honest about it. Get outside yourself today, and think only of them.

Just a Sidenote.

On top of how your kids are going to have to navigate things with divorced parents, you are going to be exhausted trying to raise the kids mostly on your own. I had a fabulous support system, but found myself emotionally exhausted at times. In my experience, the noncustodial parent doesn't help with the hard stuff very often when it comes to the kids. Yes, they enjoy their visits as long as it fits into their schedule and their new life. I realize this is not true across the board; it's simply true in my experience.

DAY 5

Talk About What Went Wrong in Your Marriage

All right, today's assignment is a bit more difficult.

Take a deep breath because I'm going to ask you to do something a little uncomfortable. At some point during the day, or this evening, I want you to sit with your spouse - go for a drive if that makes it easier - and talk about what is wrong in your marriage. What are the things that cause each of you stress? What are the difficult things that make you unhappy? What have you not talked about for a very long time? Talk about how you're feeling, and communicate that you need some things to change.

This is your chance to get it all out there. Find out if your spouse is even aware of all the things that are bothering you, and see if he or she is willing to take a shot at making some changes.

Conversations like this are difficult to have – especially once you've reached that place where you're convinced your marriage is over. But keep in mind the end goal. You may be trying to save your marriage, or you may be looking for closure. Either way, this exercise will help you start having truthful, impactful conversations. And wherever you end up, you'll be ready for it.

Even if you're saying, "I've already done this a hundred times," I want you to do it one more time.

Remember, the point of this exercise is to find out if you can possibly get back on track with your marriage. So really be open and honest with your words. Stay calm and focused. Try not to let your emotions get the best of you. I want you to think of this as an information-gathering assignment—really trying to get a handle on where your spouse is at this point.

If you can get yourself to overlook your feelings and commit to listening and hearing what your spouse is telling you, this assignment will be more successful. This isn't meant to be a spouse beating. It's meant to dig in to find the truth – the truth of what your relationship really is and if it's worth saving or not. A lot of difficult marriages start off as difficult. I have a couple of friends who dated for many, many years before finally getting married because they just couldn't seem to work out all of their problems. A good therapist helped them to see that the conflict was something they both wanted and needed in their relationship. I can see how this could be true. We are all unique and we all require different things in our lives and in our relationships. It's finding what works for us. My friends have been married for 26 years and going strong. Their relationship may not look ideal to someone else – but it works for them. And I think this is what we need to understand. This is where judgment has no place.

So, if you need to do this assignment over a couple of days or even a week or two – do it. Don't rush it if you're finding that the conversation is productive. I do realize that not everyone's spouse is going to be all in with this. You may find resistance. Listen to the resistance. It may tell you all you need to know.

Just a Sidenote.

Unfortunately, a lot of us as spouses don't really listen until it's too late and one or the other is ready to walk. It's harder at that point because you've shut yourself down.

So, if your partner is ready to listen, try to give him one more chance. If he knows you're serious, it might be the wake-up call he needs.

DAY 6

Tell a Friend What's Right in Your Marriage

Today's assignment will hopefully be a fun one for you.

Text your very closest friend and invite her or him to lunch. And if your very closest friend is your mom, great! I want you to spend that time talking with the person you trust more than anyone about all the things that are right with your marriage. Often when we're with our best friend, it's so much easier to talk about all the problems, so today may be a bit of a challenge. Stay focused on the good – 100 percent!

I'd like you to come up with at least three things—and hopefully you'll have a list that's much longer than that. Tell your friend beforehand what you're doing, and it's their job to keep you on track —no negatives allowed! Hopefully the person you're with will be able to point out some of the positives that they have observed as well.

Since you already made that list a couple of days ago of all the positives in your marriage - that should help you here, and saying these things out loud is a lot different than just writing them down. Really go for it here, and have fun! I want you to dig deep and make sure you're talking with someone who will go in the trenches with you and remind you of all the good things that have happened in your relationship. Be reminded of why you fell in love with your spouse and what made you want to be with this person to the point of being willing to marry them.

I think we all know people who simply settled for someone – maybe because they didn't think they were ever really going to find true love, or because they just got impatient and wanted a wedding or were anxious to start a family. And then we all know those couples who are so happy with each other that we find ourselves envious. What's the difference?

This is something I think about a lot because it doesn't just happen – it takes effort. It's truly magical to see two people who are giving everything to their relationship. It's intentional and it's honestly the only way to live. Today while you're doing this assignment, ask yourself if you and your spouse have the potential to turn your relationship into one that people envy. If you came together and talked about it – could you both agree to work on that? Is it something you could bring into your marriage now, or did you have it before and you lost sight of it? Have this discussion with your best friend today and see what conclusions you can come to.

Just a Sidenote.

I have two friends that I go to when I need to vent or just need a shoulder to cry on. The reason I call them is because they are the kind of friends who always point out the good or the positive, and get me back on track. They are happy, uplifting people and I love being around them. These are the people you're looking for. And if you don't have a friend or group of friends who can offer that kind of support to you – start looking for a friend like that to bring into your circle. It will be life altering.

Everyone needs a friend like this. Try not to associate too often with people who drag you down or feed your negativity. We can do that all by ourselves!

DAY 7

Reminisce Over Photo Albums

I hope you were able to have a really positive conversation from the heart with your best friend yesterday. Today is another fun day—plus it's a really easy assignment.

All I want you to do today is pull out your photo albums and reminisce a little—about your courtship, your love story, your wedding, your first apartment, your kids, your vacations, family life, special trips and events that took place during your marriage.

I think for many of us, when we reach that point of thinking we want a divorce, we lose a little perspective. It's often hard to remember all the good things that took place along the way. Because we're so caught up in everything that went wrong, we seem to sometimes bury the good – or just put it on a shelf somewhere as though it didn't ever happen. Or maybe we just want to convince everyone else that we're right. We want the anger and sadness we feel when we speak those words, "I want a divorce" to be justified. I found myself not wanting to be talked out of wanting that divorce, so perhaps we experience a bit of denial.

Grab your phone or gather up your photos, and get yourself back to your favorite spot. Get yourself your favorite treat, and start looking back on all the memories.

I said this was going to be an easy assignment, but

it may be a little hard on the emotions. So, grab a box of tissues too -- and a little chocolate.

Just a Sidenote.

Better yet, if you have unorganized photos lying around, you could make a plan to complete a new album, or arrange them with a music bed on your computer if you have digital photos.

DAY 8

Talk with Two People Who Have Step Families

If you're sticking with this, I think you're really serious about making some changes and wanting to give your marriage the best possible chance at survival, or you are serious about getting to that place of closure and the beginning of a new life.

Did you have a good day yesterday looking through all the old photo albums? I hope so!

Today is a really important assignment, so do the best you can to follow through. I want you to talk to two people today who have step families. Ask them lots and lots of questions. You want to find out about how their life is, what they are going through, what the challenges have been, if are they are happy, if they would do it again, if they wish they had tried harder in their first marriage—anything you can think of, ask it!

It's really hard to tell when looking at a stepfamily if things are working. I know from experience it's one of the hardest things you'll ever do—because not only will you deal with your own issues and the issues of your broken family, you will also take on the issues of your new spouse and the issues of their broken family. Before taking on this assignment, take some time to decide on who you plan to talk to. There are people out there in step families who have figured out how to make things work and there are others who are struggling.

That's why I want you to try and find two people you can talk to – because they may have had very different experiences.

In my own life – my first stepfamily simply could not come together during the eight years I was married to my husband. But the ironic part of that situation is that much later, I became close to my ex-husband's first wife and to his children. I'm going to talk more about this at the end of the book because I think there are some really important lessons to be learned.

But back to the assignment - really do your homework here. Take it upon yourself to gather all the information you can so you'll have something to really think about. Remember to ask a lot of questions.

Just a Sidenote.

This isn't the only time you'll see me mention this, but this is something I wish I had done before choosing to marry my second husband, and I like to suggest this to dating friends. So, consider it if you find yourself divorced and dating again.

Call up the ex-wife or ex-husband and ask her to meet you for lunch. Then ask questions. Find out as much as you can. You can discern what you need to take away from the conversation.

It's hard enough being involved in a stepfamily without knowing all of the things you should have known before you committed. Of course, you will get some information that may not be fully accurate or even true. There will be resentment and you're going to have to decide what you need to take away from the conversation. But I have learned it's best to go in with both eyes wide open.

It's interesting how men like to bring up the word "crazy" when describing an ex. And women tend to bring up the word "abusive" or "cheater" or any number of descriptive adjectives. I think it helps to meet all parties involved before deciding what is really true and what was maybe unique to their situation for reasons that don't exist between the two of you.

If you get remarried, you are going to take on a whole host of other people. Not only will their ex be in your life to a degree – but so will the ex's new spouse if there are children. And then there are the in-laws, the in-laws of the new spouse, the children, the spouses of the children, the entire extended family, and their friends. The more prepared you are for that, the better you will be. And I believe it's easier to get to know people and learn to love them BEFORE there is a wedding.

DAY 9

Ask the Opinion of Someone You Trust About Your Getting a Divorce

I hope you asked a whole lot of truth seeking and interesting questions yesterday. I hope you learned a lot of things that helped you do some deep reflection about your current situation, and also about how your situation could change – for good or bad after a divorce. You should have a whole bunch of new information to process.

Divorce will most definitely bring changes to your life and to the lives of those around you. Will those changes be bad? Not necessarily. It depends on your situation. This is what you need to be determining over the next few weeks as you work through these exercises. I'm not a big fan of divorce. But I'm also not a proponent of staying in a miserable marriage when things are absolutely not working for anyone – and when people are unhappy.

Life is just too short!

Today, I'm going to ask you to think of another person you really trust—and it should be someone different than the best friend you met with yesterday. It could be your mom or dad, your sister, a coworker, a person of faith -- just someone you trust completely that you can talk with. It should also be someone who knows both you and your spouse. I think this is important, because your chances of getting an unbiased opinion will be much greater. When someone knows and respects both people in a marriage, they will be more caring, less judgmental, and more willing to help you find some kind of resolve.

I want you to ask their opinion about your thoughts of getting a divorce. Once you've asked the question, I want you to listen! Listen to everything they have to say and absorb it. Be open to their opinion; again, this is one of those information-gathering assignments, so see it as that. Don't argue points or disagree - just listen and even take notes if you'd like. Then spend the rest of the day thinking about what that person told you.

I know this kind of exercise can be difficult, because we often want to talk to someone who will only see our side. But the point is to expand your perspective and try to see things from a different point of view.

Tomorrow is day ten, so keep going.

Just a Sidenote.

My dad begged me to reconsider when I wanted to leave my first husband. I wouldn't listen because I thought I knew better than he did. I completely refused to listen to someone else's opinion – even my own dad's. And he was one of two people in the entire world who knew me better than almost anyone. I have often thought about those conversations I had with him. I was so young and unwilling to see a different point of view.

Sometimes, people on the outside looking in truly

can help you see things you just aren't willing to look at. And if I could go back – would I have done things differently? I honestly don't know, but I do know that if I had it to do over again, I would have been more thoughtful in the way I approached things. I would have worked harder to help my husband understand where I was coming from so he could heal faster when all was said and done.

Hindsight is always 20/20. I hope that by reading some of the experiences in this book, whatever you decide to do, you will be open-minded and willing to listen to people who know and love you.

DAY 10

List Three Things You'd Like to Improve in Yourself and Set Goals

We're going to have another list-making day today. But this is a different sort of list than what you've already put together.

Today, I want you to make a list of three things you would really like to improve in yourself. Maybe you want to become more fit and healthy; maybe you want to work on adjusting your attitude; maybe you want to learn a new skill or pick up a new hobby. Whatever those three things are, I want you to write them down on paper.

And then, I want you to set some goals about how you can go about accomplishing each of those three things. So, if you want to be more fit, you could start an exercise program, maybe hire a trainer or come up with a plan for eating better or keeping sweets out of your pantry. Whatever you decide is the most important to you at this time in your life – get them down on paper. And then write down goals under each of your self-improvement items that are going to help you achieve them.

Get to your favorite spot and start thinking of what you'd like to change in yourself—not in your spouse. We're focusing on YOU today.

It's human nature that when we experience problems, we want to look outward for someone or something to blame. Even if we don't realize it at the time – we will avoid taking responsibility if at all possible. You know it, and I know it! Human nature is difficult to overcome – but it can be done – one step at a time.

So, get going on today's assignment. Write down three things you want to improve in yourself, and attach some goals to each one that will help you attain it.

Just a Sidenote.

We are all a constant, continuous work in progress—every one of us! The things you'll want to work on a year from now may be different from today's list. That's why you should review this program and do this exercise every so often to keep yourself on top of your efforts to improve yourself. But – do not beat yourself up if you fall short of accomplishing your goal. And also remember that your goals should be important only to you – no one else. Just because someone else has their own idea of what a goal looks like, does not mean it's the right one for you. So, listen to yourself and do what is right for you.

Learning new skills or accomplishing something outside of your comfort zone counts too! Sign up for a challenge – something like a 50-mile bike ride that you think you could never accomplish, or a baking class where you learn to create beautiful cakes or cinnamon rolls - and then go for it. Try. Constant improvement makes our self-confidence grow. And when we have self-confidence, we can love more completely. This is a lesson some learn a little later in life. But do whatever it takes to learn it now so you can LOVE YOUR LIFE!

DAY 11

Pick a Goal from Each Improvement Item and Accomplish it Today

How did your list come out yesterday? Were you able to narrow it down to three things you really want to improve? I hope so, because today you're going to get started on making some changes. I want you to actually do something today. Pick one of your goals from each of your items, and do it today!

If one of your improvement items is to become more fit and one of your goals attached to that is to walk two miles every day, then you're going to walk two miles today. If one of your items is to develop a better attitude and one of your goals attached to that is to smile at people more, then you're going to smile as much as you can today and make sure you smile at someone.

You're going to get out there and start making some positive changes in YOURSELF! Does that sound sort of exciting? Get yourself ready. Do whatever you need to do to get going, and get up and go do it!

I feel like making the effort to be happy and let other people feel that energy is one of the best things you can do for yourself and your attitude about life. You'll start to find that you have a direct impact on people when you do this. Think about the happiest person you know. Think about the person who everyone loves and wants to be around. Without exception, that person is one who is constantly smiling, making others laugh and helping people feel good about themselves. It's a trait we should all be working toward developing.

If you're already this person, then your goal will look different.

Don't put this assignment off. Don't wait until later when everything else is completed. Do it right now, and you'll feel great the rest of the day.

Just a Sidenote.

The idea here is to start working on forming a new habit. Do something today, but figure out a plan to keep it up. Start out with just one of your goals, and work on it until it becomes second nature before going to your next goal if you need to.

All it really takes to develop a new habit is repetition and consistency. So, commit to doing one small thing every day until you don't have to think about it any more – it just comes to you. And then go on to the next small thing.

As we all know, it's hard to develop new habits.

But it's exceptionally easy to let go of our good habits. Before long, they are a distant memory and we have to begin again. So only work on a couple of things that are important to you and don't overwhelm yourself with several changes all at once. The important thing is that you're putting in the effort and making progress – no matter how small.

The sooner you begin, and the harder you work, the less time it will take to reach your goal.

DAY 12

Write Down How Taking Some Action Made You Feel

Hopefully, you're feeling pretty good today after tackling three goals yesterday on your way to making yourself a better person. Now that you've started, don't stop! Make yourself a plan to begin progressing toward your goals, and write down what you're going to do each day. Before long, you'll be feeling better about yourself and about life.

But you can't give up!

Like I just said in the last chapter – it's super easy to let our goals slip away if we stop putting in the effort.

Today, I want you to sit down and think about how actually doing something yesterday on each of your improvement items made you feel, and write it down. Think about what you experienced, any changes you realized or reactions you had from other people—anything you can think of that made you know that you want to keep moving forward on your path of self-improvement. Did you feel happier, did you feel more motivated, did you feel like you added some positivity to your day, did you go to bed feeling better about things, were you excited to wake up the next day and do it again?

The experts say we can begin to develop a new habit after continual progress toward our goal for anywhere from 18 to 254 days –it's going to depend on the person and on the habit you're trying to form. Some habits are easier than others to develop. But the good news is – it only takes two to three months on average for these new behaviors to become automatic. So, you're going to need to keep working towards it, but that isn't really all that long! Realizing that we can be in a much different, much better place within just a few weeks to a few months is motivating in and of itself.

Easy assignment today, so get going on it.

Just a Sidenote.

In order to help you keep moving forward, I've designed a kick-start plan for you entitled "Begin to Improve in Thirty." You'll find it in a separate chapter of this book.

Take the steps that will get you well on your way to transforming yourself. This is something you can do right along with the thirty-day plan to see if you can possibly save your marriage. After all, improving things within ourselves can change our outlook in big ways, and we have to understand and respect ourselves before we can truly love someone else. I believe this to be true – and focusing more on the things we ourselves can control is always going to be the best approach to improving a relationship. Why do I believe this? Because I spent a lot of effort trying to change the men I married. And it was finally when I stepped away and began to realize I had some issues of my own that needed resolution, that I truly began to better understand relationships.

If you are fortunate enough to have two people in your marriage that love their person unconditionally and want to do everything in their power to make that person feel loved and accepted, no matter what – you are blessed. If you don't have that, I hope you can become inspired to work towards that, whether it's with your current spouse or a future spouse if you decide that divorce is the solution for everyone involved.

DAY 13

Pray and Meditate

Most people have religious beliefs in some form or another, so today's assignment is spiritual in nature. Now even if you're not a churchgoer, and even if you don't consider yourself a very spiritual person, I want you to do this assignment. It may open your eyes to things you've never considered before.

Take time today to pray and meditate. Be still and listen. Make sure you take yourself to a place where you can feel calm and be surrounded by quiet. Ask God if you are doing the right thing. Sit quietly and contemplate what a decision of divorce would mean to you and to your family. This is an exercise that really should be ongoing as you think about how to move forward in your life. So, once you've done this assignment, you may want to repeat it several times over the next few days. Divorce is such a heavy decision. It affects so many people around us, and not only do we want to be sure we're doing the right thing, but we want to make sure we're in the right frame of mind. I think that even if the decision to divorce is made, prayer and a clear head can help us move forward in the most positive way possible.

This is hopefully a way for you to take a calm approach to the decisions that lie before you. Too often we are stressed out, high-strung, and angry during the time that divorce is coming down the pike, so really do your best to take a lot of deep breaths and center yourself on what is important to you as you proceed. Think about the outcome that you envision in a best-case scenario. Even though divorce itself isn't a positive endeavor, it can have less of an impact on the people who really matter to you if you are thoughtful, careful and have your emotions in check.

Allow yourself to feel at peace today.

Just a Sidenote.

Taking as much time as you can to surround yourself with peace and quiet during this time will allow you to clear your head and organize your thoughts.

Sometimes when I really need to focus, I'll get in my car and drive to the park next to the river that is just a couple of blocks from my house. There is complete quiet and there are no distractions. Find yourself a place like that.

Once you've found yourself a spot you love – use it often. During the times when I've found myself alone, trips to the park by the river have become even more important to me. It's something that helps me clear my head, think through things before making big decisions, and realize that I am not alone in this world.

Of course, I have my kids and my friends. But if we recognize and realize that God has a hand in our lives, that He is watching over us and wants the best for us in every joy and every trial, we become stronger. We can accomplish so much more than we ever could all by ourselves.

DAY 14

Come Up with Ten Reasons Why You Married Your Spouse

I'm hoping yesterday gave you a chance to feel a calmness that you haven't been able to experience in a while. Now, hopefully you are relaxed a little bit and feeling ready to tackle this next assignment. It's not a hard one, although for some of you, it may take a bit more time to get through it. Sometimes, as the years roll on, we tend to let ourselves forget about the reasons we fell in love in the first place. This is just a chance to remember some of those special moments – those wonderful reasons that led you to say "I do" to the person you've been sharing your life with. Try to put aside the things that have brought you to this place of considering divorce – just for today.

I don't know your circumstances, so I'm certainly not saying it is completely possible to set aside the things that brought you here. For some of you, that won't be the right thing. But for others, it might be. Remember – whether your end result brings you to divorce or to reconciliation, the things you are doing now are meant to help you land in a better, healthier place.

I want you to come up with ten reasons why you married your spouse. You're going to write these down. And then you're going to ask yourself, "What did we have then that we don't have now. What have we lost?"

Make a separate list of the things that are "lost" from your marriage, and write down what you think it would take to get those things back again.

For instance, maybe you fell in love with your spouse because he or she used to surprise you with a back rub the first Thursday of every month, but you no longer get to enjoy them because, for whatever reason, your spouse has stopped giving them to you. One way to get that back again would be for you to start surprising your spouse with a back rub every so often so that he or she will return the favor. The cynical part of you may be looking at this suggestion and rolling your eyes. But honestly, it's little things like this that can make all the difference when we're trying to make amends and start liking each other again.

Have some fun with this assignment, and get your creative juices flowing. It might help you find a way to put some romance back into your marriage and fix some areas that need some work. And if not, if may help you diminish at least some of the hurt, anger and resentment that has built up over the past while.

Just a Sidenote.

You're realizing by now that this entire exercise requires something difficult. You have to try and let go of the resentment, anger, bitterness, or hard feelings that may have built up in order to get through some of these exercises. And that is the point! As I mentioned above – think about it in a way that will help YOU. If you can look at this as an opportunity to find joy within yourself – whether with or without your current spouse, you won't need to focus on your feelings about another person. This is about you making some changes in attitude within yourself. As I said earlier, if two people can each look at things from the perspective of making themselves better, happier, more resilient, more loving – both come out winners.

The bottom line is that you are working on yourself here—because you only you have control of you.

DAY 15

Call a 2nd or 3rd Marriage Friend
Ask How Their Spouse is Getting Along With Their Kids

Everybody knows somebody who's on a second or third marriage. Well today, I want you to think of a friend like that and call them up. Ask one very specific question — that's all—and then let the conversation go from there.

The question I want you to ask is, ""How is your new husband or wife getting along with your kids?"

The purpose of this assignment is to get some honest answers about relationships between stepparents and the kids. Is the stepparent really working at it or just trying to get through it until the kids are raised? Are there good relationships developing, or is everyone just being polite? And how is your friend dealing with it?

It might be helpful to talk to two different friends – one who is struggling with this, and one who is thriving.

Have you noticed lately that everyone on television, in the movies, or on-line seems to come from a broken home? And they have you believing that those stepfamilies are a dream come true. Get yourself a serious reality check right now before putting yourself in the position to someday have a stepfamily.

I'm not saying it can't work. I'm just saying it takes A LOT of work and energy to make it happen. It takes two healthy individuals who are committed to the well-being of the entire family. It takes extreme love and patience on the part of the people doing the parenting, and it takes extreme amounts of unconditional love on the part of everyone involved.

The first time I took on a step family, I was so excited! I had the Brady Bunch idea of blended families in my head and only imagined how fun it would be to add so many more kids to my family. I believed everyone would get along and everyone would love each other. The reality was much different.

Just do a little checking today—that's all I ask.

Just a Sidenote.

There are a lot of people involved in stepfamilies. Dr. Laura advised people for years not to remarry until the kids are grown. She knew what she was talking about.

It's even difficult if the kids are grown. There are just so many things to work through that you could never even imagine until you have lived it.

Again, I have done it both ways. My two oldest kids were just 5 and 8 when I married again. They wanted so much to be loved and accepted by their new stepfather. They wanted all of us to be happy and didn't want to miss a beat in their own lives. If I had it to do over – I would take Dr. Laura's advice and get them raised first. Some of the things that affected them didn't show up until much later in life, after they had become adults in marriages of their own.

The next time I remarried, I had a 4-year-old. She

was very loved by her stepfather, but when she was 12, the marriage ended and he disappeared from her life. To think that isn't going to affect a child is naïve. Of course, it was great for me – I was never going to have to deal with him for the rest of my life. But she has a hole in her heart, and has had to deal with disappointment and some abandonment issues as well. Her own father passed away when she was 21 and now she has no father at all. Our decisions as adults can have lasting consequences, and my point is just to say – be careful when your decisions are going to affect other people, particularly your children.

DAY 16

Call a Step Parent and Ask How Things Are Going with the Family

Today's assignment is similar to yesterday's assignment, but this time, I want you to call up the friend on the other side—the stepparent—and ask them how things are going with the new family.

Yesterday, you saw things from the point of view of the person who brought a stepparent into the family. Today, I want you to see things from that stepparent's point of view.

Again, you're going for complete honesty here, so you need to call someone you know fairly well, and you need to let them know they can expect complete confidentiality.

Not a tough assignment, but an important one. Be open to hearing what the other person is telling you, and try to avoid thinking it will be different for you. You may be simply amazing at relationships, but you have absolutely no control over the other people who are about to enter your life, and that means not only the step kids, but also the entire ex-family—their other parent, their grandparents, and in some cases, there might even be other stepparents and half-siblings involved! Think about that for just a minute. I am very aware of several families who are in this very situation – my own family is complicated. My youngest daughter has five half siblings – two on my side and three on her dad's side. My two oldest children have two half siblings – one on my side and one on their dad's side. But all of my kids had other step parents and step siblings come into and out of their lives.

I know a family who, with all of the yours, mine and ours on both sides – there are twelve children involved. Now the best way to look at these situations is to say the more the merrier! But it doesn't always turn out that way.

Just a Sidenote.

I have been a stepparent twice.

The first time, some of the kids simply didn't like having another person living in their house. I knew how they felt because neither did I. I didn't like who I'd become because of everything going in with these complicated relationships, and I didn't like how I treated them.

I've come to realize that being a good stepparent is directly connected to your own happiness and sense of self-worth. This is why I will harp on you until the end of the earth to get yourself emotionally healthy before you even take yourself to the place of becoming a stepparent.

By now, I've learned a few things. I became much better at being a stepparent, and it didn't hurt that I honestly loved my last stepson. He is an adorable man. It also didn't hurt that I didn't have to participate in raising him. He lives in a different state and has his own life, and he happens to like me too. Even though I am now divorced from his dad – we continue to keep a relationship.

DAY 17

Ask Yourself, "Am I Being Selfish?"

Today is one of those thought-provoking, be-honest-with-yourself, dig-deep-into-your-heart-and-soul kind of assignments.

Are you ready?

Today, I want you to ask yourself one very tough question:

"Am I being selfish?"

That's it. That's your assignment. But if you really want to do this one right, you're going to need to spend quite a bit of time today searching for the answer. Are you considering everyone and everything in this decision, or is it only about you and what you want right now?

Not an easy question to answer. But do your very best.

Just a Sidenote.

Maybe you are thinking about divorce because it is in the best interest of everyone involved. I've been in that place where I knew I had to leave, even though I was giving up everything I loved. It was truly the best decision for everyone involved! Again, I'm not advocating for people to stay in marriages where they are not happy, or where they are being abused or harmed in some way. Just dig deep and make sure divorce is truly what you want.

The point of this book is mainly to help couples considering divorce for the very first time to make sure they are very certain about their decision. And for those who are certain – I want to have an impact on how the situation is left. Is everyone talking to each other? Is everyone being supported so they can be in a healthy place coming out the other side? This includes all parties involved, not just husband and wife.

So, the question, "Am I being selfish," applies not just to getting divorced, but to staying in the marriage if that's the final decision. If you're going to stay together – there are probably things that are going to have to change. I think we could all agree that it is usually selfish behavior on the part of one or both that leads to divorce.

Thank about it – affairs, disagreements about money, sex, work habits, household chores, decisions about the children, vacations, what to watch on Netflix, what to eat for dinner, where to go for enjoyment, when to go to bed, how to divide the closet space, political opinions, religious beliefs, relationships with extended family, friends, etc., etc., etc. It almost always boils down to selfishness and an unwillingness to compromise. Most of these things are trivial, but that doesn't stop most of us from wanting our way when it comes to just about everything. And if there is one person who is willing to compromise – they often get taken advantage of by the other who may tend to be a bit more selfish.

If, in the end, you decide to stay – figure out how

you are going to compromise with each other. If you can each be more giving, you will find more joy in your relationship and honestly, in your entire life. I learned this concept the hard way, but I'm convinced the reason we live so long is because we're so hard-headed, it takes a lifetime to figure life out!

And then, once we have it figured out – well…

Work hard to figure it out while you're still breathing!

DAY 18

Ask Your Kids How They're Feeling About Things

I debated a long time about today's assignment. But ultimately, I believe it's an exercise that should be done at some point—and better now than later.

It involves your kids. If you have kids, whether they're young and living at home or grown up, I'd like you to bring them together and ask them how they are feeling about things. If they know you and your spouse are considering divorce, talk openly. Let them express their opinions freely. Make sure you listen to what they are saying and take everything into consideration. You may even want to write their opinions down so you can go over everything again later.

I'm not saying you should allow your children to make the decision for you. I'm saying they need to be heard. They need to know you care about what they think and how this is going to ultimately affect them.

Use your common sense here. If your kids are young and they don't know divorce is a possibility, talk in general terms about how they feel about mom or dad, the family situation, etc. Depending on their age, they may be more aware of things going on between you and your spouse than you think.

Get as much feedback as possible today, and really listen.

Just a Sidenote.

I feel strongly that our kids need to know they have a voice in the matter of whether or not their parents are going to keep the family together, and that their opinions matter. Obviously, the final decision has to be between the spouses – but maybe they just need to feel they are part of the decision or at least that they are able to express their feelings. I think after watching my own kids grow up without that voice, I became aware of just how important it is.

Because I didn't involve my kids as we were going through it, I've had to talk with them a lot as adults and do some apologizing. But some of the damage cannot be undone. For our family, the biggest healer has been laughter. We have always laughed a lot and found the humor along the way in tense situations. In my opinion, this is a really good way to help kids through a divorce.

If I could go back, I would be more open with them. I feel that maybe understanding some of the things that are going on will help them cope better later in life, and including them may help them work through things easier.

I had a conversation with my son recently. He is understanding and forgiving and always has been. We were talking about a particular situation and he said, "We all do the best we can with what we have at the time," and he is right. It doesn't do any of us any good to look back and beat ourselves up over something we might have handled differently if it were happening now. This is all part of our earthly experience, and it's the way we learn to be better.

I also want to say that guilt has no place in these situations. We may hurt our children or other people in our families when we go through these difficult relationship things but, at some point, everyone – including our children, must take accountability for their own lives and not use the divorce of their parents as an excuse for the way things are going in their lives. We can guide them and help them as their parents, but ultimately, they have to experience their own healing and their own forgiveness.

DAY 19

Ask Yourself, "Am I Willing to Start My Life Over?"

Today is another one of those ask-yourself-a-really-tough-question days!

And here's the question: "Am I willing to start my life over?"

One of the things I think we forget to consider when contemplating divorce is that you aren't just leaving your spouse; you're leaving your life! You may have to leave your house, you may have children who want to live with your spouse, you may have to change jobs, you will lose friends and neighbors, your activities will change, your habits will change, what you have for dinner will change—everything will change!

What you have to decide is, is it worth it?

I am comfortable with change. I handle it well. Others may not. Not everyone does. I think this is the toughest part of divorce – knowing that everything is about to change, and having no idea what that actually looks like.

Change makes us grow, and it helps us get outside of our comfort zone. But remember that your kids may not agree. Change is really difficult for kids who are invested in their lives with safe and familiar surroundings. But these are things you will need to figure out if your decision to divorce becomes a reality. I want all of these things to come into play today as you work through this thought-provoking question. Think about yourself, and also think about your family. Are you willing and able to accept the changes that are about to happen?

Know that when you do move forward – your world is also opening up, and keep your focus on looking for the good things you may be able to bring into your life.

Enough said!

Just a Sidenote.

I have started over more than once. In some ways, the changes have been good and kind of exciting. But in other ways, the changes have been extremely difficult.

And remember, things can always get worse! My mother used to tell me that all the time. And you know what? She was right! Just because you free yourself from one situation, it doesn't mean your life just became easier. It just became different.

But just so we're clear – I am absolutely willing to start my life over if I have to, and you should be too. My last marriage that I ended over eight years ago absolutely had to end! I had a great life! So great, in fact, that my husband thought I would never be able to leave it. But he didn't know me at all. I remember telling him that if the big houses, the nice boat, the trips and the money meant that much to me – I could replace them. But my self-worth, my happiness, a faithful and loving husband – those were the things that meant something to me. And leaving that marriage has been so worth it.

DAY 20

List the Pros and Cons of Leaving Your Marriage

List day!

I hope you enjoy making these lists, and I hope you're going back over them and taking the things you've written down to heart. This is a list you may have already thought to make when you first started thinking about the possibility of divorce. But if you haven't already made it, take the time today to make a really solid list.

This is a list of the pros and the cons of leaving your marriage. It often helps to see the good and the bad, side by side, written down - so you can study them and really think hard about them.

Be really fair about the pros as you think about the good that exists in your marriage. You may be having trouble with your husband, but the pros might be that the kids are happy, your house is fabulous, you live next door to your very best friend, Grandma and Grandpa feel comfortable visiting every Sunday, and your husband makes the most amazing chocolate chip cookies on the planet. Whatever those things are that you enjoy in your marriage—no matter how small—write them down.

And be really honest about the cons. Yes, I'm trying to get you to focus mostly on the positive, if possible.

But the bad needs to be examined for what it is. Just as I mentioned on Day 19, there are some things that simply will not allow you to stay in your marriage.

Just a Sidenote.

Depending on how bad the cons are, really focus on the pros. I have been in and out of marriages, but my life during all of those years has been generally good. For example, I wouldn't even have my two closest friends had I not married one of my husbands. I have wonderful children, I've learned a lot of life lessons, I've met a lot of new people, and I've had many fulfilling experiences. Ask yourself if you can live with the cons. And if you simply can't or shouldn't – then don't!

I mentioned in a previous chapter that I had a period of doubt over my last divorce and wondered if I could possibly just set everything aside, forget anything had ever happened, and just stay and start over. In my heart, I knew that just shouldn't happen. But it was when all three of my children, including my 12-year-old at the time – said, "mom, you know you can't stay," that I realized my marriage was over.

I have never looked back, and my life has been wonderful over these past eight years. What has sustained me? God, prayer, family who have offered wonderful support, my youngest daughter – who is now 23 and has been the joy of my life, friends who have loved and helped us both, wonderful opportunities that have completely changed my financial situation, and a positive attitude that keeps me happy and laughing.

The secret to a successful divorce is whatever you can find to support your new life, whoever you can keep close that makes you happy, and good hard work!

DAY 21

Make Breakfast for Your Spouse and Kiss Him Good-Bye Before He Leaves for Work

I'm going to tell you right now these last ten days will be really hard for some of you because most of them involve some type of interaction with your spouse. But these exercises are important in this whole process. Plus, I've given you a little break to look forward to on days twenty-six and twenty-seven.

I want you to get yourself up today earlier than usual, make breakfast for your husband or wife before they leave for work, and kiss them good-bye. It doesn't have to be fancy. You could microwave a pack of oatmeal or pour a bowl of cereal, but just make the effort.

Now honestly, I asked myself if I would have been willing to do this myself for someone who I felt like didn't deserve my love and care at this point. So, here's an alternative - if breakfast is a no for you, pack a lunch or some kind of fun snack the night before, and set it in his or her car, whichever you think will be most appreciated. But there is no negotiating on the kiss. Even if there have been no kisses in quite some time. In fact, especially if there have been no kisses in quite some time. A kiss on the cheek is fine.

You might be surprised at how much better you'll feel about YOU for being willing to even go here. If you can keep this as your ultimate goal – making yourself a more giving, more loving, more accepting, less judgmental, happier, more joyful person – you will be able to approach each of these assignments in a way that will make them easier. Because you are ultimately working to keep your kids feeling loved, becoming strong, resilient and accepting of the outcome – you will find the strength to do what needs to be done.

Just a Sidenote.

You've heard it said that what makes us love our children so much is the amount of service we give to them. It's no different with others. The more we do to help someone, the more love we will feel. That is just a fact. And giving affection can make us feel more affectionate.

This holds true for stepchildren too. If we are having a hard time loving or even just accepting them, maybe we could try serving them—help them with their homework, make them their favorite treat, or sit and talk about their day. It's definitely worth a try!

I'll talk more about this at the end of the book, but those difficult relationships I have had along the way with stepchildren have ended up becoming some of the best relationships of all. I think it may have something to do with the difficult experiences we went through together, but somehow, in the end, it has brought us all together. This could turn out to be true in a husband/wife situation as well. It didn't hold true for me, but you might be different. I think the reason I really like this particular exercise is that it allows you to hold the power. By taking the high road, once again you are allowing yourself to know that you have done everything you possibly could to make things right. If it doesn't happen – if you don't come back together – then so be it!

DAY 22

Hug Your Spouse Long Enough to Get a Hug Back

I hope you did the kiss yesterday! If you did, then today will be somewhat easier for you. Because all you have to do at some point today is give your spouse a hug. And if you're in the car together or sitting on a couch or somewhere in close proximity, I want you to reach over and take his hand. See how you feel at that point. And you should also see if he takes your hand back or responds in any way. Be aware of his reaction. Most likely you'll feel a bit awkward if you haven't held hands in a while. I remember some very awkward moments with my last husband when I tried to forget about things and take a risk with him.

But back to my original point – going back and trying again might be just what you need to help you realize it is actually time for you to move on. For those who are fortunate enough to truly re-connect, be grateful you gave it one last effort. And for those who are unable to re-connect – be grateful you gave it one last effort! Now you know! And now you can move on and let it go.

You are most likely going to realize it's been awhile since there was any contact between the two of you at all, and it's amazing what one little gesture like getting or giving a hug – or feeling someone take your hand -- can do for your well-being. It's true that sometimes we get ourselves locked into negative feelings about each other. We can get so caught up in being mad or disappointed that we fail to remember how it felt to be happy.

Here's an experiment to try: When you go in for the hug, try to hang in there until you get a hug back. If there is resentment built up between you, it may take a little bit, but just for fun, try and wait it out. If you get a hug back immediately, then great for you! That may tell you your spouse wants you right where you are. And that's a good thing! If the hug isn't returned or is hesitant, that may tell you everything you need to know.

Hugs and hand-holding—take it and run with it. This could end up being a really good day! Or it could end up being a day that solidifies where you have been heading. I think when we don't have our affections returned, that is something that can make the decision to leave the marriage much easier.

Just a Sidenote.

Physical contact of any kind is absolutely necessary in a husband-wife relationship. There obviously is no negotiating on this if you expect to have a healthy, long-term relationship. The less physical contact, the more distant the relationship. And the longer we go without physical contact and intimacy, the more difficult everything in our relationships becomes. I think it's really hard to have negative feelings toward your spouse if you hug a lot. But if this is something you have neglected over time – it can take a lot of humility to put your hard feelings aside and try to come back together in this way. Awkward is the word that comes to mind.

This is more about recognizing how this kind of exercise makes both of you react. Take the opportunity to observe and see what you can learn.

DAY 23

Cook Dinner and Talk About the Memorable Times in Your Marriage

So glad to see you back here today. You're almost at the end of this thirty-day exercise, and I hope it's giving you a lot to think about. But I also hope it's been inspiring in many ways and is helping you to make some changes within yourself that will affect your life in a very positive way—no matter what happens now. The decision you make about your marriage, ultimately, will be the best for you and for everyone involved – so don't be too hard on yourself. In my opinion, the person who violated the marriage in the first place is not typically the one who seeks to stay together and work things out. So, chances are you have reason to leave and shouldn't feel guilt or remorse if you choose to do so.

Tonight's assignment involves eating. Yay!

So, I'd like to talk you into cooking dinner tonight. Now, if you just can't swing it without the kids being around, then go out to dinner. But I'd like you to find some alone time tonight. You're going to sit with your spouse, eat a good meal, and talk about some of the memorable times in your marriage. The trick here is to get your spouse, first of all, to actually talk - but then to focus on some good, positive conversation. It's going to be up to you to get the conversation moving, so start by recalling a family trip you went on, or that picnic you had at the lake one weekend. Maybe you have a favorite song you used to dance to, or you can recall a joke you used to tell over and over just to laugh. Whatever your memories are, that's where you're going to focus.

Sound pretty painless? Okay, I know it's not easy, but getting where you are now has taken a lot of time and energy, so it isn't going to be effortless to try and turn things around.

This is just another chance to reconnect a little bit, so work hard to make this happen.

Just a Sidenote.

Have you ever watched people sitting together in a restaurant - eating, but not saying a word to each other?

Maybe they're just tired, or enjoying the silence. Or maybe they are in a very distant relationship. I find it impossible to not talk during dinner. So, when there is silence, I know something is wrong. Talking over dinner is a time that's great for catching up and checking in with each other because nothing else is grabbing your attention. Good food and good conversation is one of the great pleasures in life. If you can't have this with your spouse, you should work hard to find out why.

Once you start a conversation, work hard to keep it going. Of course, both people have to be willing to participate, so talk about things your spouse is interested in if he's not opening up. I think we can all agree that the more we talk, the more we start to open up about things that really matter. Give it a good try!

DAY 24

Do Something Nice for Your Spouse You Haven't Done in Awhile

How did last night go? The hope is that you are starting to reach some kind of resolve and that you're closer to making a good, solid, informed decision about what you want to see happen and where you want your relationship to end up.

All you have to do today is something nice. I'd like you to do something for your spouse that you haven't done for a while. Just something simple. You could leave her some kind of a gift, tell her you appreciate something she does for the family, or it could even be just telling her she looks nice today. Just anything that will give her a little boost.

We can get so caught up in our busy schedules and in ourselves that I think we set the niceties aside way too often. My son-in-law is so great at doing things to make my daughter's life better that I asked him to put together a list called "Thirty Ways to Love Your Wife," which you'll find later on in this book. If you're the wife, make sure you leave the page open and put it somewhere your husband can see it.

If you can get him to do those things for you on a regular basis, your marriage problems will be solved! Okay, that may be overstating things a bit, but at the very least, you will focus less on the problems.

You'll also find a list called "Thirty Ways to Love

Your Husband" put together by my daughter. So, ladies, you're not off the hook.

Okay, for today, you just have to do one nice thing; so, go do it.

Just a Sidenote.

I think doing nice things for people is more for those doing the giving. Don't you think it's fun to leave surprises for the people you care about and watch their reaction? A lot of marriages today are missing this element. Our world has become so self-centered and so one-sided that we are bombarded with messages of love yourself, pamper yourself, be kind to yourself, forgive yourself – we're leaving the people we love out of the equation. If we all only think about ourselves, we are going to find ourselves pampered and alone.

We all want someone to focus on us, give their time and energy to us, love us. If two people in a marriage can find it in themselves to focus on the other, give to the other and love the other – THAT would have us all feeling loved and cared for. THAT would be the perfect way to be in a marriage. THAT is what we should all be striving for.

Go do something nice. And then spend the next week forgetting about yourself and focusing on the needs of your spouse and see where it takes you. Don't see it as a competition or a test to see if the other person will start giving you what you want. It has to be a completely selfless act. If you're married to a taker – you'll have to decide if you can live with that or not.

DAY 25

Seek Advice from a Close Family Member

You're in the homestretch now, so keep going. Today, I'd like you to seek some advice. If you're close to your parents, it should be from them or at least from a family member who cares deeply about your well-being. It should also be someone who knows you extremely well and can offer you an opinion and advice that will truly help you. If you don't have living family members or those you can trust, look for a close friend or mentor whose advice you will respect.

Have a really open conversation with this person, and make sure you listen to what they have to say. It will hopefully give you guidance as you are making this difficult decision about your marriage and give you a few more things to think about.

You're in a tough spot right now, and asking for help from other trusted people in your life who know you extremely well and know your situation can ease some of the burden. So, take some time today to go visit or call your parents or whoever you choose to confide in. Tomorrow's going to be a fun day.

Just a Sidenote.

Looking back, If I could have a do-over, I might take it!
I would at least be open to listening to my parents'

advice and really thinking about their opinions that, by the way, were based on experiences they had been through. Why? Because I know now they knew me better than I knew myself; Because I know now they had my best interest at heart; And because I know now I could have possibly saved myself a lot of pain. More importantly, I could have saved my kids a lot of pain.

Life is something we have to experience. We don't have all the answers, and the things we go through are all part of our individual journey to help us become better, stronger, smarter. Hindsight is always 20/20 and I think we have to lay that aside and realize we made the best decisions we could at all times in our lives. Yes, we would all do some things differently given the chance, but accepting our decisions and learning from the experiences those decisions bring is a healthy way to live. Whatever you choose to do going forward – do it with conviction. And then do the best you can with what comes across your path. Make your decision and accept the next chapter of your life.

I don't believe in holding on to regrets or guilt of any kind. Life is way to short for that! I believe we all do the best we can with what we have to work with at the time. That said, I also believe we can learn from each other's mistakes, and that's exactly what I'm trying to achieve – I'm hopeful my own personal opinions, based on my experiences, will mean something to some of you. That they will perhaps inspire you to think beyond what you know today. But in the end – this is about you and your personal journey. Use this book in whatever way it can help you – no judgment!

DAY 26

Create an "Escape" List

I promised you a few days ago that you could expect a little break. I'm calling it that because I think today and tomorrow will be fun, relaxing assignments that will allow you to realize that you can and should be taking care of yourself—not just during this time, but all the time!

So today, I want you to think of some things you could do to "escape" when you're feeling stressed. These should be things that you really love to do or things that make you happy. Maybe you like to light candles and take a bath or read a book, or maybe it relaxes you to work in your garden. If you're a guy, maybe you want to watch football or go do some fishing—just whatever it is that makes you feel you can get away from it all every so often.

I made a conscious decision long ago to figure out the little things that take me away, that make me feel happy and that I look forward to and get excited about. I turn to those things whenever I can to help me remain in a positive frame of mind.

Write these things down, and keep your list somewhere you can refer to it often – like in your phone. I think we actually forget to do things for ourselves. I can be really good at this sometimes, but then the business of life gets in the way and I'm back to trying to remember to enjoy life more. We forget that we can take some alone time and re-energize. Work hard on this, and come up with a really good list today.

Just a Sidenote.

Just for fun, I've written up my own personal "escape" list later in this book. You can use it for inspiration if you need help making a list of your own.

DAY 27

Take an Hour and Try Out One of the Ideas on Your "Escape" List

All right, how does your list look? I hope you have several things on it that make your heart leap just a little bit. These should be your absolute favorite alone-time activities. And as you think of more things you could do, add them to your list!

So today, I want you to take at least an hour—longer if you have the time—and try out one of your ideas. Yes! Does that make you happy? Today, you get to spend some alone time and do whatever it is that will make you feel relaxed and energized. So, pick your activity for the day, and then go do it! This is about you today and realizing that you can take control of your own life and do something that makes you happy.

We all have so many demands placed on us. If we don't take time out once in a while, we end up sending ourselves into overload, and that's not a good place to be. I know because I've been there many times!

So, go have a blast with today's assignment.

Just a Sidenote.

I have had to learn to relax over the years and teach myself that it's important to take time out. I feel so much healthier and happier now than I did when I would run myself into the ground and never stop! You may need to learn the art of relaxing as well.

That said, everything in life that becomes important to us must be a priority in order to remain in our life. That only makes sense. I often think life is a rollercoaster. Sometimes we are doing everything right, and at other times, life can get in the way and push our priorities to the back of the line. And you know what? That's okay.

Sometimes we have to let things go for a while as we prioritize other things or work on what's more important at the time. And then when things settle down, we get back into the routine of doing those things that remain our priorities.

This has been true for me throughout my life. There are times – like now because I started a new job this year – when I have to remind myself to have fun. I have to remember that life is not all about work, so I have to schedule fun on my calendar. Because if it's on my calendar – it will get done.

Escaping in the form of physical activities, spending time with the people we care about, going to lunch with friends and even taking road trips or vacations need to be scheduled just like everything else. That's why creating an escape list of simple pleasures that can be done on a whim or spur of the moment are so important. It's a way to have fun and enjoy life without having to go to the effort of planning or creating something that is going to be a big deal or take a lot of time.

If you haven't been doing this already – make fun a priority in your own life!

DAY 28

Talk with Your Spouse About the Well-Being of the Kids

I hope you're feeling great today after taking some time to yourself yesterday. Just remember to let yourself escape every so often when you feel like you're in need of some alone time or relaxation time—it will make you a better, happier person. Just ask my family!

Now today is one of those difficult conversations that needs to be had with your spouse. You need to get outside of yourself again today and focus on the kids. I want you and your husband to sit down together and really talk about the well-being of the kids. How are things going right now with contention in the house? How might things work if the two of you were to actually divorce? If you have grown kids, how will this affect them? How will it affect your future relationships with them? What about your future grandkids? Are you willing to split your time with them? I want you to really get into the nuts and bolts of this.

There are a lot of things to consider when kids are involved. Not only will they be torn having to go between homes and parents, but their schedules and activities will also be affected. They will most likely feel sadness, and they may eventually have to deal with new people coming into their lives.

This is where it gets really rough. And whether your kids are very small or full-grown, there are still going to be issues. This is no small thing. Try to have a really deep, serious, intense conversation today, and see what you can come up with between the two of you. You are both going to have to live with a very different set of circumstances if you do decide to divorce. Now is the time to determine if it's something you can both live with and also work through together for the good of the kids.

Tomorrow is your last difficult assignment, so get back here tomorrow ready to take it on.

Just a Sidenote.

No matter where the two of you wind up in the end—together or apart—this is going to be a healthy conversation, and one that needs to be had.

Divorced parents who can put the kids' needs ahead of their own are way ahead of the game in the long run.

I have had a pretty good relationship with my first husband over the many years we have been divorced. He married a wonderful woman who loves my kids and works hard to maintain a relationship with them even now that they are grown. We were able to sit together at band concerts and programs, attend events and be in the same room together, talk about the kids when necessary, and work out any issues that would arise. When my daughter and my son had their weddings, the day was very comfortable with all of us there together.

I am grateful for that. As fun as it sometimes feels to feud with the ex and his new spouse, it's not good for anyone involved, especially the kids. It's so much nicer if everyone can just get along.

DAY 29

Clear the Air, Apologize and Take Responsibility for Your Own Failings in the Marriage

You made it to day twenty-nine—way to go! Now even though this is going to sound hard when I first tell you what you're going to do today, it will feel really, really good once it's over. Does that help?

Today, after everything you've been through over the past twenty-eight days, I'd like you to find time to talk with your husband or wife and clear the air—apologize and take responsibility for your failings in the marriage—and let them do the same.

It's amazing what an apology can do, for the one receiving the apology AND for the one doing the apologizing. In some cases, maybe it will bring you both to a point where you want to keep trying and stay together. If you do end up getting divorced, an apology will help make the transition a little smoother. It will hopefully help the two of you be able to get along better and even stay friends in the future, which is most definitely the best thing for all involved. And of course, the hope is that if you offer an apology, you will get one in return. It's always a two-way street, and we all have something we need to offer an apology for - if we're being honest.

You've done a lot of hard assignments in the past several days, and you can do this one too.

Meet me back here tomorrow one last time for day thirty. You're going to ask yourself one last question and spend the day or maybe several days contemplating the answer.

Just a Sidenote.

Leaving things on good terms is the best-case scenario if you can do it. I think this is one of the most important days of all in this exercise. Saying you're sorry and taking responsibility will give you both power – whether that's the power to dig in and work harder, or the power to walk away and wish each other well. If it doesn't keep you together, it will most definitely help some feelings heal as you begin your lives apart.

I think this kind of communication can help in the long run and I say that because before I separated from my second husband – we did this. It wasn't easy, and not everything that was said was positive. There were tears, and there were accusations, but it cleared the air.

We were able to eventually come back around and be friends – for the sake of our daughter. And I know this one thing has been extremely helpful in helping her live a healthier life. A few years later he became very ill with cancer and dementia and spent the last two years of his life in a facility. My daughter was serving a mission for our church in the Philippines for 18 months, and I would go visit him and let him talk to her when she would call home. He was so appreciative and so was our daughter. After she returned home, I would go with her to visit him for the next year until he passed away. I am so grateful that we both had the ability to put the past behind us and stay connected until the end. It meant the world to our daughter. And honestly, it helped me heal in a way I would not have imagined. We may not want to stay married to someone, but it doesn't mean we have to hate them or treat them with disrespect.

DAY 30

Ask Yourself One Final Question, "Is a Divorce What I Really Want Now?"

You stuck with it and made it to day thirty, and I am so proud of you. I know it hasn't been easy. But life-changing activities never are and frankly, they shouldn't be!

Now for your very last day. I want you to ask yourself this one final question, and consider the answer throughout the day. Here's the question: "Is a divorce what I really want now?"

You may need more than one day to think about your answer, and that's fine. Truthfully, you've most likely been pondering this question for a very long time. You should take all the time you need when you have a decision like this to make. I hope the activities you've completed over the last thirty days have had some major impact on your thought process, on your attitude, and on your behavior.

Just a Sidenote.

I really hope these thirty days have helped you clear your head and put you in a better place in your thought process. The fact that you're trying to work through things says a lot about you as a person.

The purpose of today's activity is twofold. It's meant to help you not only in your decision-making process

– is divorce the right choice or is marriage what I truly want -- but also in your quest to become a better person.

If you have friends who are considering divorce and this exercise has been helpful to you in any way, I hope you'll refer them to this book. I've had different reactions to it. I have most definitely had people tell me this book helped them as they made their decision. I've had couples say they worked through the exercises together. I've known couples who worked through the 30 exercises and decided to stay together, and also those who have chosen to move on. I had one woman tell me her husband was not willing to do Day 1 and, needless to say, they divorced. I even had one upset woman call me to tell me that she thought I was carrying guilt and wanted to make her feel guilty for wanting to divorce – which is not something I can help another person resolve.

But I assure you I do not judge anyone - ever. If there's one thing I've learned through my journey, it is that we all have our own crosses to bear. None of us can understand what another couple is experiencing because our situations are all very unique. We all have our own set of very interesting and challenging problems, and no one can tell us what we should or shouldn't do.

You are the only person who can make the decision for yourself and for your family. But I'm hopeful that you will use the tools available to you to make the most informed, most thoughtful decision you can.

CHAPTER THREE

DIVORCE MEANS CHANGES AND MORE CHANGES

I'm pretty good with change. I actually like it!

I would probably be diagnosed with some kind of "desire to pick up and change everything when you get bored" disorder if I were to see a therapist. My life has been full of them. When it's time to repaint, I simply sell and build a new house.

I'm kidding. Sort of.

But with each divorce comes some kind of change or move. And whether I was able to keep my house, or was forced to start completely over -- at some point, circumstances changed and a move was required.

For me, this has been an adventure.

For my kids, not so much.

Here's the problem with having to move so many times when you have kids. Their stability becomes affected. They have to move away from friends, and when you're growing up, friends are one of the only things that really matter.

My daughter, who is grown and married, will tell you that her biggest issue with moving so many times was that even though I kept them in the same school, they now didn't live near those kids they went to school with, so their friendships faded.

This is how the moves and marriages looked for me and my kids over the years:

I built a darling house with my first husband when my son was eighteen months old.

I divorced my first husband when my son was three and a half years and my daughter was three months old.

I sold that house when my son was five and a half and my daughter was two and moved a short distance away to a bigger house that was out of the school district. But my son had already started kindergarten by then, and I didn't want to disrupt him, so I would drive him to my parents' house before work, and they would take him to school. Luckily, they lived a block and a half away from the school.

But the house was too big for the three of us, and I wanted to live closer to my parents and the school, so I built my third house as soon as the other one was sold. I loved this little house! It was perfect for the three of us, and we were in a new neighborhood with a lot of other kids around. We were living back in their school district, and everything was perfect!

But I didn't want to stay single. I married my second husband when my son was about nine and a half and my daughter was six.

I sold that house, and we moved into a "temporary" condo with my new husband, where we stayed for nearly four years. I kept driving the kids to their same schools even though we were now living in an adjoining city.

Then we sold the condo and built a house in the same city, but a bit of a distance from where we were living. The kids were in fifth grade and ninth grade, so we decided to change schools at this point. My daughter loved her new elementary school and made friends quickly. She is the type of person who will not let others exclude her, so she worked like crazy to fit in.

My son was now going into a new high school with brand-new kids he didn't know. He made friends—not good ones in some cases. But he loved high school and got involved in the band with his drumming and did very well academically.

But the truth is that neither of the kids really ever fit in with a solid group of friends. We moved into a well-established area where everyone already had their longtime friends, and there just wasn't any room for someone new. It was a very difficult time for them. A lot of families move around and relocate and do just fine with new experiences – and that's not to say a lot of the experiences we all had weren't really positive and good for us – they definitely were. But it's somewhat different when divorce is in the mix and parents aren't together. I tend to look for and notice second marriages where the parents really work hard to accept everything about their new situation and make it work for everyone. Those scenarios absolutely do exist!

By the time my teenagers were nineteen and fifteen and a half, I divorced my second husband. And now I had a new two-year-old added into the mix. My ex-husband stayed in the house this time. Because we were so far in over our heads, no one could afford the payment. He eventually lost the house and I was even more grateful I had moved on.

I built a new house in a neighborhood across town, and the four of us moved in a few months later. Again, I loved my new house and my new neighborhood. But I stayed just two and a half years before I remarried again!

This time I sold the house and moved to the city where I had been working and commuting to for years. It is forty miles away, so my daughter who had just graduated from high school decided to find her own place at this point and stay and go to college. My son was nearly twenty-two so he was already living away from home.

I took my four-and-a-half-year-old daughter and moved with my new husband into a beautiful new house that we bought together. This was going to be my forever home, and I believed we would stay there permanently. I loved the neighborhood so much. We lived within walking distance of the bike path along the river, across the street from a beautiful golf course.

I met five of my closest girlfriends – all with children around Gabby's age, and it was the most perfect place for my daughter to grow up.

I loved my husband and was in this marriage for the long haul. But we don't always have control over the things that happen. When my daughter had barely entered junior high school, I got the heart-wrenching news of my husband's first affair. Others would follow. Cutting to the chase - I was "allowed" to stay in the house until my daughter graduated from high school, and that was the deal I took so that she could have that consistency in her life. It was not a fair settlement, but it helped me achieve the most important goal for my daughter and myself. I was able to save the money for a down payment on a new house, and we moved a couple of days after she graduated closer to where she would be going to college. She lived at home with me for the first year and has had an amazing life since then. She is graduating this year from University and she fulfilled an 18-month service mission in the Philippines as well. She is 23 and thriving. And I am so very grateful that I have been single this entire time! That time raising my daughter, bonding with her, living my own life, working hard to build back and having a thriving career have been entirely worth it.

It makes me exhausted just going back over those details and remembering all the moves and all the changes. It's no big deal when you're alone. But when you drag kids into the whole thing, it gets very, very complicated. And the thing is, you really never know what you're going to get when you enter a second or third or fourth marriage. I always tell people it's a crapshoot once you leave your first marriage. Maybe that's just me. I'll admit that my last marriage had red flags waving boldly before me from the very beginning – and I ignored them. But I did not see some of the things coming in my other relationships. And honestly, sometimes, two people simply bring out the worst in each other.

The men I married were decent men in a lot of ways. But the baggage and the sadness and the bitterness and the responsibilities and the angry kids and the ex-wives and the money issues and the generation gaps and the set-in-my-ways mentalities and the awful furniture and the nasty habits—they can all add up to failure in many, many cases.

Putting your kids through all the crap WILL affect them – whether you want to admit it or not! And I have friends who have entered wonderful second or third marriages to amazing men. But there are still going to be things to deal with. My best advice is to be prepared for whatever comes your way. Be mature enough to protect yourself and your kids. Be kind enough to accept your new spouse and everything that comes with him. You CAN make a new marriage work – but it DOES TAKE WORK!

My oldest kids, for the most part, have come through all of this all right. But the biggest reason for that is because they had grandparents who lived close and loved them. They were a stable, consistent entity in their lives. They had a support system that allowed them to grow up and be healthy adults – albeit not entirely. They still have some long-standing struggles. Had I not had that support system, I am honestly not sure where they would have ended up.

Before you make any kind of decision, ask yourself if you have a strong support system.

There were moments when it was touch and go. Those teenage and young adult years were scary sometimes. They both headed off in directions, for a time, that were not healthy. And yes, kids who live in stable homes with two parents who stay together for the long haul can still head off in unhealthy directions. But with divorce, you're almost guaranteed at least a few challenging problems with your kids.

How do I know this? Because I have lived it – a few times over! I've had many friends who have lived it – and some have done it beautifully!

A lot of kids move on a regular basis because of their parents' employment or for other reasons. And they grow up just fine.

But when you add stepdads and different houses and neighborhoods, and new friends all at once, it can be really hard on everyone. Kids need stability in their lives. Mine had their grandparents and their same school. Figure out what the elements are that you can keep constant for them and do everything you can to protect their sense of security.

Yes, change is a good thing!

But not when you're messing with your kids' lives and sense of self-worth! Make the changes adventurous and help them know they are loved at every turn. I know for myself, when I was really young and getting that first divorce, I was not the most selfless mom. I loved my kids but wanted less responsibility. My parents picked up that slack. Hindsight.

CHAPTER FOUR

LIVING WITH MULTIPLE MARRIAGES AND DIVORCES

If you were to talk with my two older kids about what it was like moving around all the time and living with two different stepdads, they'd tell you it wasn't easy. The thing is, they always kept good attitudes about it, which made me think they were all right. But the truth was, they were just trying not to rock the boat.

Think about that for a minute.

In reality, they were suffering. But my daughter will tell you she knew I was stressed and worn out most of the time, and she didn't want to burden me with her own problems. She and my son made a joint decision to keep their own issues to themselves because they thought I had enough to deal with.

My son finally found it in himself to tell me what he thought when I announced I was thinking about getting married for the third time. He was twenty-one at the time, and he laid it right out on the table. There was no holding back on his part, and I was hurt and upset by it at that moment. But looking back, I'm glad he was able to tell me how he felt. It was healthy for him to be able to just get all of that bottled-up frustration and anger out in the open for all of us to see. But he wasn't just frustrated that I was getting married again. He had no respect for the man I had chosen. He saw things that I did not see – and I thought he was wrong. I listened to my son, but I definitely did not want to hear him.

It didn't change things for me. I still went through with the marriage. My daughter said at one time that she was closer to my third husband than any of the others who had been in and out of our lives. That's the part that began to bother me so much. My two daughters truly loved him. And yet, he was able to betray us all. Which means – my son was exactly right about him. I was bothered because ultimately my daughters were hurt deeply by his disregard for us.

So, what do you do? Keep trying until you get it right?

I do have faith in relationships. I do have faith that real love exists and that two people can come together and make each other happy. And I will most likely try again.

Be prepared for a time in your life when one or more of your kids reach a point when they grow up and feel they may finally tell you how disruptive to their lives your choices have been. They can finally put their feelings out there for you to hear. I'm telling you from personal experience that you'll wish they could have done it sooner. You'll finally realize how they've been feeling all those years, and you'll see what they've been through. Most importantly, you may wish you would have done things a little differently.

My kids have grown up to be wonderful adults who are successful in many ways. But getting there has been a real journey for them. My oldest daughter is strong in a lot of ways, but she has had her emotional struggles. I like to think she never had a moment worth of pain over these past years, but that simply isn't true. She and her husband have had to be very deliberate about how to approach marriage. Is that a bad thing? Absolutely not! They have been married now for many years, and they are determined to work through their problems.

My son had a much rockier path. He was married at 28 to a beautiful woman, but there were several years where I wasn't sure he ever would get married. Marriage has not been easy for them, but they love each other and they are determined to work through their difficulties as well.

He grew up without his dad in the home, and for a boy, that's a really big deal. Any good therapist will tell you that boys, raised by their single mothers, are at a disadvantage because of too much love and not enough discipline. I spent a lot of time over the years worrying, crying and taking grief from husbands who loved my daughters, but merely tolerated my son. And, in my experience, this is not unusual.

I have several friends who have experienced a similar thing. It appears to be easier for a man to love a stepdaughter, but maybe the competition is too great with a stepson. This is a very big thing to consider before getting remarried. Make sure there is genuine friendship and concern for your sons before you choose to bring another man into their lives. I'm absolutely not saying that all men are like this – I'm saying this has been my experience.

And women, the same may apply to you. If you find it hard to love a man's daughters, please reconsider.

I can only imagine, as I look back, what it must have been like for my own kids and for the kids of the men I married. I had never been through those experiences as a kid. My parents remained together for their entire lives. But I would assume that all sense of security, comfort, unconditional love, and happiness fly right out the window with every change that comes along.

My daughter says kids are resilient, and that they can survive and conquer these kinds of changes. While that may be true, I want you to consider the kids in every move you make. That's why I feel so passionate about this topic – whether you choose to stay married or get a divorce, do it in a way that will help the kids understand, feel loved and feel safe – with both of you, their parents. We all know this logically, but putting it to practice in real life can be a challenge.

And if you can't possibly put your marriage back

together, think about staying single until your kids are grown and moved out. This obviously won't be right for everyone, but I wish I would have been able to consider it. Both of my adult kids were married by the time I was forty-nine years old. I'm just saying that I was still young. Waiting until then to pursue a relationship would have been completely all right. But then, of course, I wouldn't have my beautiful daughter, and I can't even begin to imagine life without her!

If you're considering divorce, start making your plan. Write your plan in the form of a letter or contract to yourself. Frame it and hang it on your wall! Bronze it and put it where you'll see it every single day of your life! Do something that will force you to really think through the details.

I didn't have a plan. I flew by the seat of my pants for several years and found myself in a crazy place as far as relationships go. But I love where it has landed me now and can honestly say I wouldn't trade any of my experiences – good or bad.

There are so many different types of circumstances and relationships out there, and there are some who are able to make step families work, for sure. I have one friend who married a man I thought, at first, was an odd match for her. But as I got to know him, I realized she married him because she knew he would be a good stepfather to her kids. He had never been married. She has seven kids. Who would have thought that could work out? The kids seemed to love him, and he appreciated having a family. The marriage lasted for a few years, but ultimately, they parted ways. Her kids have remained close to him though, and I think that's great for them.

I have friends who have been married as many times or more than I have. I have friends who have hard marriages and friends who have great marriages. It's difficult to know just exactly what makes for a lasting relationship – but selflessness, honesty and trust have to top the list. I spend a lot of time these days observing marriages and learning from them.

Speaking kindly to and about each other, touching and holding hands, supporting each other, talking and kissing, doing thoughtful things for each other, playing together, there are so many wonderful things that can happen in relationships if we will commit to each other and focus on what we can do for each other.

Second, third, fourth marriages are not easy. Most of us think being married to our first spouse is hard until we are in a position to compare - and then we may find out we had it pretty good.

But never give up hope - no matter your decision, and no matter where you find yourself – never stop working toward having a solid, happy relationship with a wonderful human.

CHAPTER FIVE

SELF-IMPROVEMENT

With regard to my first marriage – for the few years afterward, I asked myself, "Did I give up too quickly?" And my answer to myself for several years was…

Yes!

Looking back, I tend to like blaming my decision on the fact that I was exceptionally young the first time I entered into marriage. And this is true. I was just about to turn nineteen when I made that life-long commitment. I was too young. By the time I turned twenty-five, I was a very different person who wanted very different things out of life. However, it was no excuse.

A lot of people marry at a young age and make it just fine.

But I was one of those people who needed to grow

up a lot before making that kind of promise to another person. Still, I went through with the marriage. Looking back, I realize that I should have done everything within my power to make it work. Why? Because I made promises to another person. Because I had two beautiful children whose lives were entrusted to me and their father. Because marriage is serious business and not something to be taken as lightly.

I left too easily.

But, on the flip side, I was unhappy in my situation and was excited about the possibility of a new life, and I simply could not get myself to rethink it.

What could I have done to make myself consider things from a different perspective?

I realize now that I had a low self-worth at that time in my life. I'm not entirely sure why. I've never tried to be analyzed by a counselor to see why I do the things I do. But I have learned over the years that making myself the best person I can possibly be is the number one ingredient to a successful marriage. Why? Because at least if you're happy with yourself and you like the person that you are, you can possibly overlook a lot of the things that are making you crazy.

If you're happy with yourself, you can contribute rather than take away from your marriage.

I've dedicated the next three chapters to self-improvement because I've come to realize, in my own experience, that making myself better is all I have control over. I cannot fix the person I choose to marry – none of us can. I can't make them be this way or that way.

I can't require that they make changes for the good of the marriage. I can only require that I make changes for the good of the marriage.

So, let's talk about self-improvement.

I think we can all agree that there are five areas where we all need to be focused and working in order to be healthy. We need to constantly be looking at our spiritual, emotional, physical, mental, and intellectual well-being if we are to be well-rounded individuals. Doesn't this seem right?

Let's take a moment to talk about each of those areas.

FIRST, **spiritual health** is different for each of us. We need to determine as individuals what we consider important to our spirituality. Some of the things we might consider are the following:

- Believing in God or a higher power
- Attending church
- Praying on a regular basis
- Being in tune with our surroundings
- Feeling a spiritual connection to other individuals
- Committing to and being converted to a religion
- Realizing and accepting that we are all God's children

Work hard to understand who you are and what you believe and go from there. Make a list of the areas you need to improve. Consider the things that will make you stronger spiritually, and work on attaining those. If you want to commit to a religion, explore your options. If you need to work on gaining faith that God exists, talk with others and do some research. Do the things that are going to bring you in line with where you want to be.

For me, my religion is a lifestyle. I'm a member of the Church of Jesus Christ of Latter-Day Saints. And when I'm not being true to that lifestyle, my entire life feels out of whack. Spirituality, for me, is at the top of the chart because without that, I can't move forward in other areas.

Decide where spiritual health is for you, and work to make yourself better.

SECOND, **emotional health** is, without a doubt, the one thing that can bring every one of us down if we haven't worked to sustain it and improve it.

In the next chapter, you are going to read about ways to improve your emotional health. I have listed the things that I find are a good starting point. And after a bumpy ride in your marriage or a decision to divorce, you may very well find yourself in need of some strategies that will help you arrive back to a place of emotional well-being.

Let's look now at some of the things we might consider in this area:

- Looking for ways to feel secure in who you are
- Not worrying about what others around you are thinking or saying

- Finding ways to know you can handle challenges
- Figuring out what makes you like yourself from the inside out
- Knowing you don't have to settle for second best
- Building your self-confidence to know you can do anything

These are just a few thoughts off the top of my head of things I know contribute to my own emotional sense of well-being. None of us are going to have our emotional health intact at all times throughout our lives. We are constantly a work in progress, which is why we should consistently be checking in with ourselves to see where we're at.

It is impossible to be happy and to move forward in life if our emotional health is not in check.

Take a look at yourself, and decide what you need to do to improve your emotional health.

THIRD, **physical health** is a huge plus! Getting yourself in top physical condition and eating good, healthy food will simply make everything else you do easier.

I have tried to maintain some kind of exercise throughout my life. But there have been times—during my last year of college, for a while after the birth of my last child, during a job that had me waking up at 3:00 a.m. five days a week, after hip replacement surgery—when I have had to let it go. And oh man, did I pay for it!

Once you've been fit, you almost can't deal with the idea of being overweight and flabby. It's just not in your DNA any more. And when you have to give it up, for whatever reason, it's not good for your physical, mental, or emotional health.

If you could do better in this area—and most of us can—let's consider some of the things we might look at to improve:

- Working out on a regular basis
- Eating healthy fruits and vegetables
- Eating lean protein and whole grains
- Cutting back on sugar, oils, cheese, and foods that put your health on alert
- Stopping unhealthy habits like smoking or drinking alcohol
- Drinking more water
- Dropping a few pounds

Let's face it: When we feel better physically, we can perform our daily tasks with ease. Our outlook on life and the way we treat others improves greatly, and we feel happier because we are healthy.

And the bonus is that when you maintain a healthy body weight, you just look better. You can wear anything you want because clothes look good on you. And that just makes life a little more fun.

There are just so many reasons to get yourself physically fit, it shouldn't even be an argument you have with yourself. Just go do it!

FOURTH, **mental health** is one of those things that is hopefully a bit easier for most of us to maintain. It's basically how we think, feel, and act as we try to cope with life. However, some of us may have trouble during stressful periods actually coping in a healthy way, and we may have difficulty relating to others and even making decisions and choices.

I know I've had periods of major stress in my life where I thought I would literally go crazy or lose my mind. But I think we all feel that way at times. It's when you really are in danger of being unable to cope that you should be concerned.

It's possible that intervention by a therapist or counselor may need to come into play if you're finding you just truly can't deal with the events in your life. Our mental health is so important to our overall well-being. We need to do everything we can to stay healthy in this area.

Some things to consider might be the following:

- Seeing a therapist or counselor regularly or as needed
- Taking steps to reduce the stress you are under
- Finding out what personally helps you cope
- Learning to change the way we think about certain things
- Seeking advice from others who could help with decisions or choices

- Surrounding yourself with friends and family so you don't feel alone

Mental health is as important as emotional or physical health. I believe if you are taking care of yourself in all of the other areas we've talked about, your mental health will follow. If it doesn't, it might help to seek help from a therapist.

FINALLY, there's **intellectual health**. Our intellectual health refers to our ability to think and learn from life experience. Some of us may be a little slower in this area than others. Yes, I may be referring to myself here. You know how most of us insist on learning everything the hard way… Maybe you can relate.

It's a bit more than that, however. It's being open to new ideas, being able to evaluate information, and knowing how to utilize your own resources to expand your knowledge and improve your skills. Did you know that common sense is part of our intellectual health?

Let's consider some ways that will help us improve in this area:

- Learning to use our common sense when making decisions
- Considering different ways of doing something
- Learning to be resourceful so we can make things happen
- Figuring out how to use our past experiences in making future decisions

- Finding ways to improve the skills we have
- Finding ways to challenge our minds and bodies
- Increasing our desire to learn more and acquire knowledge
- Figuring out how to handle problems

There is much we can do to improve our intellectual health. Feeling healthy in this area can make us feel capable, competent, and successful. The more knowledge we have, the more skills we acquire; the more challenges we give our minds and the more resources we learn to use, the more confident we will be in our own abilities.

You can see that finding a healthy balance in each of these five areas—**spiritual, emotional, physical, mental and intellectual health**—will make us well-rounded, healthy individuals who can conquer most anything.

The challenge is to always be working on something in each of these areas. We may be at places in our lives at times where we are spiritually and physically on top of the world, but lacking in the emotional or intellectual categories. Or we may have it made as far as intellectual or spiritual health goes, but we have more work to do to improve our physical well-being.

Finding balance is truly the key.

Now once you've brought yourself to a place where you're working diligently to improve your overall health and you're doing everything you can for the good of the marriage - but the issues your spouse has are not being dealt with, what do you do?

You have a few choices:

- You can divorce your spouse and head out on a new "adventure."
- You can talk to him or her – heart to heart - and try to motivate the changes.
- You can bring a third party in for counseling or coaching.
- You can leave him or her alone for a period of time and wait to see if something will motivate the changes to begin.

You already know this by now, but you only have control over the things you decide to do and the changes you decide to make. If you love your spouse, look to the future and ask yourself if you want to be in this marriage twenty years from now.

Ask yourself if you believe things can improve. Remind yourself that you are making changes in yourself that will affect the health of the marriage. If you can be patient, you might see things begin to change. But commit to giving it time. We are all human, and none of us can change overnight. Real change takes real effort.

And it would be irresponsible not to bring up the fact that sometimes people can and do change… for a short period of time, as was evident in my experience with my last husband.

If those changes are not motivated from a deep desire within oneself to change for themselves, they are certainly not going to make those long-term difficult changes for someone else. They are not going to make them for you. Part of my point in writing this book is to help you determine for yourself if you or your spouse can make the necessary changes to make your marriage successful. I had gone back in hoping for real change. For the first five months, I began to think it was actually possible. But in this case, I was wrong.

No matter what your circumstances are, no matter what your problems in the marriage are, never forget that change begins with you!

CHAPTER SIX

WHAT ABOUT YOUR EMOTIONAL HEALTH?

If we're completely honest with ourselves when things aren't going well in our personal lives and we're having trouble getting along with our spouse, we're not really emotionally healthy during that time. And it takes time to recover from every incident we go through. For some, this can be a day-to-day struggle.

As you continue to work on your relationship, if that is what you have decided to do, it would be a big plus if you could get really serious about your own emotional health.

So, I'm going to help you do that in this chapter. I've outlined "Ten Steps to Emotional Health" so you have some place to start. As you read over these steps, you'll see that it takes a bit of effort to get ourselves in a different place. It doesn't just happen.

After my first divorce, it didn't take me long to be back into a relationship. Why was I so anxious to be with someone?

I have asked myself this question many times in my life: "Why am I so anxious to be in a relationship?" I have come to realize that, for me, at least early on in my life, I loved the idea of being in love. That's a really hard thing to admit, but some of you may see yourselves in that statement. The problem is that when we can't be alone, we rush into something that may not be right for us. And then - when the going gets rough, we get going onto the next.

I bring this up because not only has this been a difficult thing for me personally, but because I have known so many others who have done exactly the same thing.

I have come to realize that part of the ease of moving on comes from choosing men who are easy to leave—men who have issues and baggage themselves, who we know in the deepest part of our hearts are not good for us and are not men we truly want a long-term relationship with. That way, when it's time to move on, we don't have to make excuses.

Think long and hard about that if you see yourself here at all.

For some, choosing a good man is just not as exciting as choosing a man who needs a little fixing. And for some of you men, choosing a needy woman is much more exhilarating than choosing a stable one. Sound familiar?

Why do we do this? I'm only speaking from my own experience here, but after watching my own pattern over the years, I have concluded that when we don't take the time to work on our own emotional health and get to a healthy place BEFORE getting married, we are actually attracted to the broken people who are just like us! Could this be true?

Ask yourself, at this point, if you see yourself potentially in the last five paragraphs.

If you do, in the end, decide to leave your marriage, will your life play out as mine did? Will you jump from relationship to relationship in search of that perfect man or woman who can make your life better? Or will you be the one who decides to get yourself back on track and move ahead in your own life before bringing someone else into the mix?

Are you beginning to see just how important your emotional health is?

Then let's break out the list:

Ten Steps to Emotional Health

1. Reconnect with your family.
   They'll be your greatest support system.
2. Let your friends help and support you.
   Ask for and accept their help.
3. Talk with a counselor or divorce coach to get some direction.

4. Get enough sleep.
   But also get yourself out of bed early and start moving.
5. Spend some time crying.
   Allow yourself time to feel sad for a short time and let your emotions out.
6. Do your best to stay positive.
   Don't talk about your problems or bash your spouse to your friends.
7. Get out and go for a walk every day.
   Enjoy and appreciate nature.
8. Focus on others' needs for a while so you don't become bitter.
   Helping others will help you forget about yourself.
9. Write your negative thoughts down in a journal so you can purge them.
10. Work hard to get your life back together.
    But make sure you take opportunities to escape.

This is a pretty good list! But it's not all inclusive. Figure out where you are lacking and add some things in that will benefit you. It will get you focused and give you some direction so you're not just out there grasping at anything and everything that you think will make you feel better.

I have known several people who have absolutely lost themselves either while in their own marriage or after a divorce. And it takes a while to get back on track once you've let that happen. If you don't like my list, make your own. But put it in writing, and then actually do the things on the list. The point is to get yourself moving in a positive direction and doing things that will contribute to a healthier attitude and outlook.

I know a person who stayed in a bad marriage for the kids. He knew things weren't good, but the day his wife called him to tell him she'd been having an affair and wanted a divorce, he was devastated. Because he hadn't taken the time to work on himself during the marriage, he was a wreck for the next two years until the divorce was finalized. He was lonely and sad, couldn't work, couldn't function in a healthy way. And he jumped right back into a marriage that is even more difficult than the last. He didn't work on his emotional health then, and he isn't doing it now.

It's important to have direction during these really hard times in your life. It's normal to have feelings of hopelessness, loneliness, loss, and even apathy during hard times in a marriage. But the trick is not to let those feelings take over your life. The list will help save you from self-destruction if you read it and follow it!

Another concept I have found to be very helpful during stressful times in my life is finding ways to escape once in a while so I can relax and calm down. Actually, I've made it a habit now to always find time to escape—even when I'm in less stressful periods of life. That might be taking a short road trip over the weekend to see friends or spend some time alone. It might be taking the time to get a pedicure or a massage.

SHOULD I GO BACK

I even see taking a bubble bath at night a really great way to escape.

Sit down and make an "escape" list of your own - the things that help you relax and make you happy.

I'm sharing my own "escape list" with you just to give you some ideas because, let's face it, some of us just don't know how to relax, and we need some ideas to get our brains thinking along those lines.

The things on my list are those things I love to do. They are the things that I look forward to and reward myself with after I have done the things that must be done.

Keep in mind while you're creating your list that these should be things that are close by and easy to escape to. I used to love spending time on our boat, but it was six hours away, so putting it on my list defeats the purpose. These should be "quick" escapes that take no thought and will give you some much needed relief when you need some time to yourself.

I can think of a couple of people I know who, had they decided to help themselves learn to enjoy time alone, may not have felt the need to remarry, myself included. Sometimes we think we can't be alone. But I'm telling you, being alone and having time to yourself is an absolute treat. Learn to see it that way, and you'll enjoy your life more—whether you stay in your marriage or decide divorce is the answer.

So, take my list and then create one for yourself:

1. Working in my greenhouse.
   I do not have a green thumb. But I love

being outside, getting my hands in the dirt, and I also love vegetables straight from the garden. One day I decided I'd like to try my hand at gardening. I assembled one of those inexpensive greenhouses so I could start learning. The first year, I grew absolutely nothing. Literally everything died! But the second year, I figured out some things and read up on the subject. And most things lived! I was able to plant some vegetables in my garden and enjoy them well into the late fall.

This year, I'm expanding my greenhouse to include flowers. I love being outside taking care of plants and inhaling the garden smells that overwhelm me when I'm working.

My greenhouse has done well so far, but some of my problems along the way have included my puppy stealing the plants once they were in the garden. This didn't get me too upset because I loved that puppy – but seriously?! And I've also had to learn how to maintain the greenhouse so that the elements didn't destroy it.

I'm figuring out how to solve problems, and I think that's a good thing for anyone at any age.

2. Cooking.
   Cooking actually used to stress me out! It's

one of those things that got me thinking, "I have to do this every day—all the time!" It bothered me that it was something I didn't particularly like doing.

I wanted to learn to love it, so I started watching Food Network. I fell in love with Barefoot Contessa and bought one of her cookbooks. Then I started buying some decent cookware and knives and things that made cooking easier and more fun. And then I bought more of Ina's cookbooks, and then Joanna Gaines' cookbooks. I've learned to cook more simply with healthier ingredients from my garden, and it has since become more of a pleasure for me. Now that I'm living alone, I can choose to cook anything I want – only food that I love and prefer. When my daughter comes home on the weekends, she always teases me that there's no food in the house. She means there is only healthy food… Haha.

3. Relaxing in the hot tub.
   I used to have a hot tub in my backyard, and I would often go out and use it after my youngest daughter had gone to bed. Sometimes, I'd even sneak out there in the middle of the day if it was raining, because I think it's just so cool to be outside, soaking in the hot water, while it's pouring rain. It

was covered and private, so I could really relax. A hot tub for me is total relaxation. And, as a bonus, it helps me sleep better. I gave up my hot tub when I moved, but have plans to get another one now because it's something that really makes me happy.

4. Reading by the fire.
   I have an animal-print chair and ottoman right by the fireplace in my house. I love sitting in that spot. I usually read books just before I go to sleep, or on Sunday afternoons when I just enjoy the slow peaceful quiet time. But when I really want to just chill out and not think about anything, I'll grab one of my favorite magazines and curl up with a blanket.

   Confession: It's the curling up by the fire that I really love here, not so much the reading.

5. Taking baths.
   I really love taking baths. And it doesn't matter what time of the day it is. If I need to escape, I'll light some candles, turn on some good music, pour in some delicious bubble bath, and sometimes pamper myself with an aromatherapy masque.

   It works every time!

6. Surfing JCrew.
All right, this one's kind of an indulgence – okay it's a time waster - but I love doing it, so I do! I like to surf the J Crew website to see what inspiration I can get for putting things together that I already have in my closet. I like to look for new ways to wear something or new ways to pair things together. Plus, I love just looking at the fabulous clothes and shoes!

And yeah, I shop it sometimes too!

7. Taking naps!
Almost every day, I take some kind of nap. When I was in college, I used to run home around noon and take a fifteen-minute power nap every day. I had it down to a science. I could lie down on the couch, be asleep in a matter of seconds, and automatically wake up fifteen minutes later.

Before my three puppies passed away, I'd cuddle up on the couch with a blanket and all three of them. Heaven!

8. Watching scary movies.
I know it doesn't sound like much of an escape, but it's true. I love a good scary movie! Most people I know think I'm nuts, but if I happen to be home all alone one night, I'll climb in bed early and watch a scary movie.

It may not sound very relaxing, but it is certainly an escape and a treat for me.

My older kids understand because they do it too! When they were growing up, it's something we used to do together. We love it!

9. Ordering takeout.
   I love eating out in restaurants, but a good take-out meal makes me happy when I'm on my own! I have a list of favorites, and when I'm home alone for dinner, I'll run out and bring something home (like a strawberry salad, a burrito bowl or some tomato-basil soup), pull my coffee table close in front of the television, get comfortable, and thoroughly enjoy my food while watching a good series on Netflix.

10. Sitting on the deck.
    In warmer months, I love to sit out on my deck and eat breakfast or sip a Diet Vanilla Coke. Just sitting out there in the yard when it's beautiful and peaceful makes me feel calm and so relaxed.

The idea of having a list like this is to get yourself thinking about ways to bring more periods of happiness or relaxation or stress release into your life. I know I'm a much easier person to be around when I know I always have things like this to look forward to.

I absolutely need things to look forward to often in my life. And you do too. I think it helps each of us cope with whatever we're dealing with, plus it just makes us happier people.

And isn't finding happiness our ultimate goal?

Get going on your own "escape list."

1.
2.
3.
4.
5.
6.
7.
8.
9.
10.

CHAPTER SEVEN

BEGIN TO IMPROVE IN THIRTY (30 DAYS, 30 WEEKS – PICK YOUR OWN TIMEFRAME)

I believe if we all took a serious look at ourselves, we would come to realize that not all of our problems are caused by someone else. We are each responsible for deciding how everything that happens to us will affect our lives. The way we react to everything—good or bad—is up to us.

Let me stress again that each of us only has control of ourselves. If we choose to stay in a difficult marriage, we have to decide if we can be happy in that marriage regardless of what the other person is doing or how they are acting.

We all know the reason marriage is so hard, is because when you take two people - who each have their free agency - and bring them together, the outcome may not always be exactly what you were hoping for. We are all individuals, and we are all on our own journey in this life. I believe we have to be willing to let each other live his or her life. And we can only hope and pray they choose to live it in the best interest of the marriage.

That being said, I want to stress how important it is for you to work on your own self constantly so that you are contributing to the marriage in a positive and productive way. Doing that will have more impact on the way the marriage functions and may eventually motivate your spouse to take the same action.

I created the following list I like to call, "Begin to Improve in Thirty." I created it as sort of a sidekick because I think it's hard to work on your marriage when you're drowning in your own issues.

Here's the list. It's sort of a kick-start plan to help you in your efforts. I'll meet you on the other side of it, and we'll talk more:

1. **Write down the three things, in order, that are most important to you in your life.**
    1.
    2.
    3.

    Obviously, there are going to be many things that are important to you, but these are your most important, wouldn't-want-to-live-without, can't-even-think-of-not-having-these-in-my-life things. So really think on this one before you make your list.

Maybe it's your kids, maybe your faith, maybe money. These three things will most likely be consistent with your values, but whatever they are, write them down.

2. **Assign a goal to each of your three things. If you listed family, maybe your goal could be to hug each family member every day.**

The idea is to actively do something every day that will bring your important thing closer to you and allow you to give it the attention it deserves.

3. **Decide on three things you can do for yourself that will make you feel better. Maybe exercise an hour a day, or cook a healthy dinner at least four times a week.**
    1.
    2.
    3.

Maybe health isn't even your issue. Maybe adjusting your attitude is what you need to do to make you feel better. Think outside the obvious, and dig deep to figure out what it is you really need here.

4. **Take some action. If you said exercise an hour a day, then buy some exercise DVDs or new running shoes; do one thing for each of your items that will help you make it happen.**

   You are setting goals here and working toward making them happen. Write down what you are going to do so you don't get sidetracked.

5. **List five things you'd like to learn—a language, gardening, computer skills, etc.**
   1.
   2.
   3.
   4.
   5.

   I always have a list written down of new things I'd like to learn even if I know I don't have time right now. I like to have a list for the future. Having things written down in a place where you can see them keeps your mind working all the time.

6. **Now take one step toward accomplishing each of the five things you'd like to learn.**

If you said learn a language, then sign up for a class. If you want to read more books about American history, buy a book or download one. Do whatever it is that will get you one step closer to your goal.

You may have time right now for just one of your five things, and that's fine. Keep the other four things on your list for the future.

7. **Think of three people you know who need some kind of help, and write their names down.**
    1.
    2.
    3.

These could be members of your own family, or they could be neighbors or coworkers. The purpose here is to think of other people besides yourself. If you're already good at doing this, then good for you!

8. **Now write down one thing you are going to do for each of those people to help them.**

It could be something simple like picking up the leaves in their front yard or taking dinner in one night. Or if you have time, it could be something ongoing like offering to take their garbage to the curb each week.

9. **Do that one thing for each of the three people you listed who need help.**

   This exercise will make you feel so good about yourself that you may find you want to keep looking for people who need help. Nothing takes us outside of ourselves the way service does.

10. **Take five minutes and tell each member of your family what you appreciate about them. And tell them that you love them.**

    This is a quick one-time exercise that will hopefully make you want to take five minutes each week and point out something you appreciate that was done to help out the family that week. This one might drive productivity within your family and get your kids motivated to help out more often.

11. **Devote fifteen minutes each day to praying, meditating, and contemplating your life, your goals, your plans, and your desires.**

    I think we get way too bogged down with the details of our daily lives, and we forget to stop and be grateful. We need time each day to pray and think about our goals. Take this one very seriously. It could change your life.

12. **Think of a topic you'd like to know more about—maybe how to start your own business—and research or read something about it every day.**

    This assignment will keep your mind sharp and will help you start thinking of the new goals you want to set for yourself in your new life.

13. **Do a thoughtful service for someone without them knowing.**

    You could do this for a member of your family if you want. My daughter started a game where she did something nice for one of us and then left a little stuffed animal with a note that says, "Now you do something nice for someone and pass this on." It kept us always thinking of something nice we could do for one another.

14. **Make the decision to get out of bed a half hour earlier each morning.**

    Even if you just wake up early and stay in bed reading a book or snuggling the puppies or using the time to be quiet and think about your upcoming day, it will reduce your stress level and allow you to clear your head before you start rushing around.

15. **Put a time limit on the amount of time you watch TV, surf the Internet, or text.**

There's a fine line between relaxation and time wasting. I have to consciously decide to shut it off and go do something productive after I've watched my favorite show or shopped on my favorite site.

16. **Go through your house (room by room) and deep clean and declutter.**

This is one of my favorite things. I love cleaning and organizing my pantry and my closet two or three times a year. Plus, I like keeping my entire house clean and neat. I think a clean house makes for less stress and a sense of peace.

Sometimes though we have to let the house go when we have a lot going on. Go ahead and take a break. Just don't stress about it.

17. **Think of that one person in your life who drains your energy, and take steps to eliminate that person from your daily life.**

I have had to do this more than once in my life. It's one of the hardest, yet one of the best things you'll ever do; whether it's a good friend, a love interest, a husband, a boss - it has to be done if you want to remain a healthy person.

I once had to tell a friend I couldn't be her friend anymore. She was constantly asking to borrow money and rarely contributed anything productive or positive to our friendship. Just seeing her was beginning to affect me to the point where I just had to let that relationship go.

And twice, I left jobs very quickly because of controlling and disrespectful bosses. Don't beat yourself up for letting people like this into your life; just make sure you do something about it when it happens.

18. **Write down ten things you could do to lower your stress level—deep breathe, listen to music—and do one thing from your list every day.**
    1.
    2.
    3.
    4.
    5.
    6.
    7.
    8.
    9.
    10.

I've got this one down pat. Over the years, I have been in a lot of stressful situations just as you have. I know by now what helps me relax. You have seen my list and have hopefully worked on one of your own. Also, I don't necessarily love working out, but I do it because I know that over the long haul, it's what makes me feel like an energetic human being who can accomplish all of the things expected of me.

Find your magic list, and make time for something every day.

19. **Decide on the one thing you would most like to change in yourself, and set three goals toward accomplishing it.**
    1.
    2.
    3.

It doesn't matter what it is as long as it's something that's important to you. Write your goals down, and put them somewhere you're sure to see them every day— like the bathroom mirror. This is one of the most empowering exercises you will do if you follow through and make it happen.

20. **Consider getting a dog; they can make you love more, feel calm, and even lower**

your blood pressure (I had three until they died passed away, one by one. I like to joke that I had one for each divorce…)

I have said many times that had I discovered the joy of having dogs sooner, I might have saved myself from a marriage or two. Seriously, they have brought loads of happiness into my life and my family's life.

21. **Make a list of ten things you like about yourself, and keep it where you can see it.**

    This is a list only you will see, so be honest about it, and make it good. Sometimes we feel we should only see the improvements that need to be made, but we need to learn to love ourselves and see the good as well. So, if you like twenty things about yourself, make a list of twenty things!

22. **Make a list of the top three places you'd like to travel to. Start by creating a plan for your first trip even if it's a few years away.**

    I have planned to go to Europe for many years and have finally booked my very first trip to Italy this Fall. I am taking my best girlfriend with me. She is married, but her amazing husband is letting me borrow her for two weeks. We are so excited making our plans. It has made my whole year having this trip in my future.

1.
2.
3.

I have a list of the ten trips I'd like to take before I die. It gives me something to work for and something to look forward to. Make your own list and start figuring out how you can make it happen. Your list doesn't have to be over the top. In fact, one of my plans is to rent a convertible and drive the West Coast.

23. **Tell each person in your immediate family you love them every day.**

Sometimes we take the people we love the most for granted. Tell those people you love them often. I try never to hang up the phone from talking to one of my kids without telling them I love them.

24. **Think of the one chore you despise, and stop doing it! Mine is ironing; that's why we have dry cleaners.**

Do you agree?

25. **Get a new hairstyle or a new outfit—something that makes you feel fabulous! Guys, maybe a new golf club ;)**

    Even if you just pick up one piece—a new top, a new necklace, or shoes—pick something in a color that makes you happy (something you love that will put a spring in your step and make you feel good when you wear it). This is a time in your life when you need to treat yourself on occasion. And you don't have to spend a fortune doing it.

26. **Start smiling more; become very conscious of it.**

    When you smile at another person, they will almost always reciprocate. And I don't know about you, but that makes my day! When people smile at you, it gives you a lift and makes you feel like you have friends in the world.

    So be the first one to reach out, and see how it can change your life!

27. **Say hello to two people you don't know every day.**

    It's a little awkward at first when you're not used to speaking to people you don't know, but then it gets to be really fun. Just make a point of saying something to the person standing behind you in line or someone passing by you on the street. I promise this one thing will make you feel happier!

28. **Find something to laugh about every day.**

Whenever I need a good laugh, I call my big brother. We can talk on the phone for a really long time and laugh about 90 percent of the time. I always remember the time I left my dad sitting at the airport waiting for his plane. He was wearing his entire suit, white shirt and tie – because he didn't want to pack them, and on his feet… his white tennis shoes so he could walk through the airport. It struck me so funny that I called my brother to tell him about it. It took me awhile to even get the story out because I couldn't stop laughing. We were crying tears of laughter and could barely breathe. I love laughing so much!

Find someone in your life who has an infectious laugh and a great sense of humor, and make sure you call him or her more often. If you don't know anyone like that, look for someone, and make that person your new friend!

29. **Get out and get some fresh air every day—go for a walk, work in your garden, or sit on the porch.**

    This is just pure common sense. Getting out in the open each day, especially in the warmer months, can refresh you and make you remember all you are blessed with. Get involved in your surroundings, and take advantage of the things that are close by you.

    One of the things I love to do is sit on the deck when it's raining outside. Thunderstorms in the spring are my absolute favorite, and I look forward to enjoying them when I can.

30. **Think of your dream—that one thing you wish you could do! Start researching and taking notes. See if it's possible for you to achieve your dream. And then take steps to go after it!**

    The reason for this is so that you have something you're always working toward. Having a goal or a dream keeps us excited about life and gives us hope for the future.

    Pull your dream out of the back of your head, and write it down. The sooner you start doing something about it, the sooner it will become a reality!

Now just so you know, this isn't a list you can complete in thirty days! It's a list of thirty things you can do in any order, over any period of time that works for you. In fact, I like to keep this list handy because if we're truly trying to improve ourselves and our lives, we should constantly be thinking of ways to do that. And we should actively be working every day on something, anything that will push us closer to our goals.

There are many things you could add to this list to make it your own; this will simply get you on your way to thinking about and seeing things in a different light. Step out of your comfort zone and start trusting yourself. Your confidence will build as you are able to mark things off your list.

The purpose of this list is twofold: First, it will allow you to start focusing on the things you need to do to begin feeling good about yourself again. And second, it will get you outside of yourself so you can stop thinking about your problems and work on all the good stuff!

This isn't a perfect list – it is simply a starting point, a place for you to begin feeling inspired. Use it. Change it. Throw it away and start over. But do something TODAY!

CHAPTER EIGHT

CAN YOU BE HAPPY IN A DIFFICULT MARRIAGE?

What do you think? Is it possible to be happy in a difficult marriage?

I know plenty of couples who are in difficult, or even downright unhappy marriages. I think we all do. I know married couples who have separate bedrooms. I know couples who are technically married, but living completely separate lives in different houses. I even know someone who has been separated from his wife for nearly five years – living in his own apartment with no intention of ever going back – yet, still married.

This all likely sounds pointless to a lot of us – me included. Why in the world would a person stay in an unhappy, unfulfilling marriage?

Well, I think people can have any number of reasons for putting up with a less than happy relationship and staying in the marriage.

For instance, I am generally a happy person. My three marriages did not define who I am, and neither does your marriage. We all take our individual selves into a relationship, and even though we may be having trouble in our marriage, we are individuals and still have experiences of happiness that may have nothing to do with our spouse.

For example, I met some of my very best, closest friends when I was married to one of my husbands. Had it not been for that marriage, I would not even know these two women. And at this point, I couldn't imagine my life without them in it. My associations with them during the marriage and now, after the marriage, have been extremely happy times for me.

I certainly wouldn't have my kids had I not been married to a couple of my husbands. When things were very stressful with my relationships, I focused on my kids.

My oldest daughter and I used to go out for French fries once a week; it was our little escape and something we did together. If we were home alone, we'd make nachos or chocolate chip cookies together. She'd make taco soup and we'd enjoy it together.

I know – It sounds like all we did was eat under stress. But this is just one of the things we did to spend time together.

My son used to work for the movie theater, so he'd take me to a movie once in a while because we could get in for free.

My daughter plays the piano, and she used to compete, so I kept myself involved in her music.

My son plays the drums, which meant I'd go to all the high school football games, basketball games, concerts, parades—anything and everything he played for. Those things made me happy.

My youngest daughter was a high school cheerleader – once again, football games, basketball games, parades. I was involved in her school. She'd have friends over to our home for parties.

I spent time working on my career. I've reinvented myself a couple of times, and I like focusing on new ideas that will keep me busy and productive.

I finally got myself some puppies—something I should have done much earlier.

I have always kept up on my exercise. I change up what I'm doing so I don't get bored, but staying fit is something that makes me happy and keeps my outlook positive. Plus, it doesn't hurt that clothes look better on our bodies when we're trim. I'll admit I sort of started taking it easy on myself for a while because I was telling myself I don't need to work that hard at this age! But I have definitely changed my mind now because the older I get, the harder it is to keep in shape! I've been working with a trainer – something I've never done before. And it's been amazing. My health and my strength are something I want to keep intact going into the last phase of my life.

Working on hobbies or looking for new hobbies is also a good way to keep yourself happy.

And if you're involved in your church, that's something that allows you to get outside of yourself and focus on others.

Let's talk about friends.

I always make time for good, uplifting friends. We go to dinner when we can or call one another on the phone. We need friends, especially when we have trials. If that's not something you've found important in the past, reconsider.

As I've already mentioned, I like to keep a list of new things I want to learn when I have more time. It keeps my mind focused on growing as an individual. It helps our peace of mind and our state of happiness to have things to look forward to.

Of course, we should all be taking time to relax and escape a bit during times of stress.

And finally, I love movies, so I collect them and watch them in bed when I have time.

Now let me point out that this is not, in any way, a list of ideas to take the focus away from your marriage or away from your husband. It's simply a survival list—things you can do to take the focus away from problems or difficulties you may be having in your marriage currently.

It's also a list of ideas that will make you a better half of the equation, and that can only lead to good, positive improvements in your marriage.

I've said it before, and I'll continue saying it, but keep in mind that you can only control what you do to make your marriage better. It is up to your spouse to decide when and how to make necessary changes that will be for the overall benefit of your marriage.

Whether you are in a marriage that you have decided to stay in long term, or even just until the kids are raised, depending on the kind of problems you are dealing with, these ideas can remind you that you can choose to be happy in a difficult marriage.

Some may be in marriages that are having serious problems, but maybe you will see that over time, there is hope for coming back together. Maybe you're doing everything you can, but you're waiting for your spouse to get to the point of realizing he has to put in some effort too. If you are choosing to stay, I'm telling you that you can be happy during that waiting period.

Don't give up.

I've heard it said that if you're having problems in your marriage, wait it out for five years. Most marriages will get past that bumpy spot and be able to work things out. It is very possible to get back to being happy.

Is this always true? NO!

There are things in marriages that should not be tolerated. And there are also things to consider other than the children. When one of you is significantly unhappy, or when you just can't find a reason to stay together – sometimes it's just best to move on. This is my opinion, and I make that known. I believe life is too short to be miserable. Each of my marriages broke up for different reasons — selfishness, serious money issues kept secret, long-term affairs. These are not usually things that can be resolved over time. I know some people are able to come back together and forgive — that's great! But for me, I don't feel that it's necessary to continue in a marriage when there have been incredible amounts of betrayal.

Every marriage and every couple are different. Each must choose for themselves, and there are a lot of different elements that go into a decision like this.

What I'd like you to gain from this chapter is this: Don't run away too fast.

Don't throw in the towel until you have exhausted every strategy, every effort, every idea you have. Why? So that you will have resolution. So that you will know you did the right thing when all is said and done. You never want to look back and say, "I wish I had..."

Remember, problems exist in every marriage, in every relationship. Yours is not different. If you leave this marriage and eventually decide to enter another, you will have problems and challenges in that one too.

I was talking to a friend recently who is married for the second time, and she said, "I've learned that it takes ten times more energy to make a second marriage work. It would have been so much easier to just fix what was wrong in my first marriage." More on this in a later chapter.

She is right on!

Could this be true for your marriage? Is it possible to fix what's wrong?

Think about it.

CHAPTER NINE

THIRTY WAYS TO LOVE YOUR HUSBAND

My oldest daughter has been through marriages and divorces with me since she was three months old. She had two different stepfathers. Because of that, or maybe in spite of it, she is so completely committed to making her marriage work; she's nearly obsessed with it.

She created this list of "Thirty Ways to Love Your Husband" to provide a fun way for every woman to creatively look for ways to make a wonderful, solid connection with their husband. We all want to feel loved, and as women, we can sometimes lose sight of the fact that husbands need to be reminded too that we love and appreciate them.

SHOULD I GO BACK

When she and her husband first married 14 years ago, they had several issues to work out. And why wouldn't they! After all, her husband's parents were separated multiple times throughout his childhood, and you already know what my daughter experienced. Like many of us, they could have just given up and moved on. But instead, they pulled it together and made a conscious decision to do the things that were going to make them both happy.

They are a happy couple and work hard to prioritize each other. We can all learn from them. Do they and will they continue to experience problems and challenges during their marriage? Absolutely! Just because they have it together now, doesn't mean everything will fall into place for the rest of their lives. And this is true for all of us. The ebbs and flows of life and marriage. But they are taking their knowledge and building on it. They are taking their life experiences and using them to their advantage. They are taking the tools they have created and writing them down so they can refer to them constantly. They are realizing that marriage takes work, and they are working now to stay solid!

So, take this list, and think through it, ladies. Do these things as much as you can, and add your own items to it. It will possibly change your life for the better!

1. Be patient.
2. Pamper him.
3. Have sex!
4. Have the occasional night apart.

5. No gossiping.
6. Respect your spouse.
7. Counseling is an option.
8. He can shop too.
9. Be thoughtful.
10. Look at yourself before criticizing.
11. Make a list of what you love about him.
12. Be the "cool" wife – play with him, give him friend time.
13. You are not his mother.
14. Think of him as your boyfriend.
15. Allow some off days – you don't always have to be on your game.
16. Have a late night once in a while – stay up late, be intimate, and cook food.
17. Be healthy.
18. Keep your tongue under control.
19. End relationships that take away from your own relationship.
20. Don't roll your eyes at his hobbies.
21. Turn off the electronics.
22. Have a weekly check-in.
23. Stop thinking so conventionally.
24. Make a financial plan.
25. Get away together.
26. Show interest.
27. Make him feel like your man.
28. Help maintain family relationships.
29. Schedule and organize.
30. Realize this is hard work and commit to it.

I love this list. My daughter was just twenty-four years old when she created this list. Her ideas are insightful and meaningful. And that is obvious because their marriage is fourteen years old and counting.

Those of us who have been through divorces or difficult marriages may find ourselves a bit jaded. So, I think it's good for us all to listen to advice from a younger person who has experienced so much and come through it so well.

Take this list and use it! It's meant to keep you thinking and to keep you from slipping into a comfortable routine with your husband.

CHAPTER TEN

THIRTY WAYS TO LOVE YOUR WIFE

My daughter married a good young man, and she loves him from the bottom of her heart. She will be the first to tell you that he is the reason their marriage is strong. He has always treated her with respect, and he knows how much the little things matter. As I watch the two of them together, I'm so grateful that she was able to find someone who deeply cares about her and about making their marriage work.

They are both completely committed to each other. I personally have learned a lot from them, which is why I asked my son-in-law to share his list of "Thirty Ways to Love Your Wife."

You may be familiar with the way Dr. Laura teaches women to care for their husbands and all will be well. But my son-in-law is proof that it works both ways. He is the one who started caring for his wife right from the beginning, and it has paid off for him. I wanted to share this list with you, so here it is:

1. Listen to your wife.

My wife can come to me at any time and talk to me about anything.

Why wouldn't I want to hear about her day or her concerns? If you take the time to listen to your wife, and be sincere about it, she will do the same for you. I let my mind wander sometimes when she's talking, and she can always tell. She can also see it in my face when I'm ready to die from boredom because I'm not all that interested in what she's saying.

The lesson here is to give your wife your undivided attention when she's talking. You will be a much happier man in the end.

2. Money matters.

It's never worth it to argue about money or let it get in the way of your happiness; this is the quickest way to damage your marriage.

My wife and I have discussed our money goals, and we're currently working together to save more and be debt free. We're working on not wasting our money. Our student loans seem to be growing and growing, and our living room still doesn't have that sixty-four-inch flat-screen TV with surround sound, but we're constantly working on being financially stable.

We've talked about falling on hard times, and we're learning to be more frugal in our spending. If tough times do come our way, we've made a conscious decision to remember we still have each other, and lack of funds will never be a reason to have an argument.

3. She has skills too!

Compliment her when she does something good or achieves a goal.

This sounds easy, but I think many of us forget to compliment her special qualities and celebrate with her when she does something great. There was a time when my wife was working really hard at becoming a Turbo Kick instructor, and she dedicated a lot of her time to reaching this goal. The time finally came for her big test, and I knew that day was important for her whether she passed or failed. I met her at the end of her long test day with some flowers and a big hug and had dinner all planned.

She passed, and we celebrated. This was a great opportunity to express how proud of her I was.

4. Take care of her when she's sick.

When she's sick, go out of your way to help her feel better.

Make sure you have all the medication she needs, and make sure she gets plenty of water. Help her be in an environment where she can sleep. Be her nurse. I wouldn't suggest purchasing the busty-nurse Halloween outfit, but if it helps her recover, then go for it. You being there for her will help her recover.

Women rarely whine or complain when they are sick, unlike most men who make a simple head cold seem like the Ebola virus. I know I'm guilty of this exaggeration of symptoms.

5. Make her feel like a woman.

She wants to feel like a woman, and you're the best person to make her feel this way. She doesn't need to feel like your little princess because she's not your daughter and you're not her dad.

She needs to know that when you look at her, you see an amazing woman who you think is so beautiful you just need to tell her from time to time. Be creative. I don't just tell my wife she's beautiful; I look for ways to let her know how much I love her and how much she means to me. This is where I like to use the fifteen-second kiss. It's unexpected, and she's normally swept off her feet by it because she didn't see it coming. At least I like to think so. After about fifteen seconds, stare in her eyes, and tell her just how beautiful she is.

You'll want to avoid garlic previous to trying this out.

6. She needs security.

Be by her side every step of the way, and be protective of her.

Women are attracted to guys who can make them feel comfortable and secure. If you're considering hiring a rent-a-cop to follow her around, I'm not sure this will help. You are her security. When you're there for her, she feels safe.

My wife was involved in a very hard internship at a substance abuse clinic and was finding it hard to not bring her baggage home from work. I could feel this when she walked through the door. She would try and act like she hadn't had a rough day and that it hadn't emotionally drained her, but she's very easy to read. I needed her to feel comforted when she came home from a day like that, so I made sure to greet her at the door with a big hug. One night, I had chips and salsa waiting for her on her side of the couch.

Security comes in many forms, but her trust in you and your ability to make her feel calm and at peace is the greatest security you can provide.

7. She needs time with you; you need time with her.

Remember when you two were first dating? I do. After that first date, I needed to be with her every day, and she felt the same way. Granted, the occasional break was needed, but I wanted to be around her, and she needed me to be there with her. Now that you're married, has this changed?

For us, we openly express this need and do all we can to still spend whatever time we can with each other. Through life's struggles and hardships, I've learned just how much I need her there for me. I was recently going through some unexpected medical challenges, and who did I have by my side providing encouragement and helping me all the way? My wife.

8. It's good to have a men's night out.

I've talked a lot about being there for each other and spending as much time with each other as possible, but let's face it; we all need a break from time to time.

I like to meet up with my best buddies once a week and just hang out. This is time away from my wife and home, and it's healthy as long as it's not obsessive. She'll understand when you say you're going to go watch a ball game with a friend and you'll be home late. She should do this as well. It gives both of you some time to yourself.

Hopefully, you'll find yourself excited to go home because you've missed your wife.

9. Pamper her.

Learn how to give an awesome massage.

If you claim you're a terrible masseuse, and that's why you can never do it, then you're missing out on one of the greatest experiences in life. Go online. There are plenty of videos and referral sources out there to help you learn how to give a good massage. Really, it's just your touch that she wants.

If you really don't like massaging, then save a little extra money. Instead of buying that new Xbox game, put it toward a one-hour professional massage. Or purchase a manicure or pedicure or anything else she loves.

I'm definitely not the world's best masseuse, but I certainly give it a good try.

10. Respect her.

As a man, you demand respect, but do you deserve it?

I hear men bad-mouthing their wives quite often while at school or work. This kind of behavior shows just how little some men respect their wives. I've had predicaments where someone at work is bad-mouthing his wife, and as I'm passing by, I'm thrown into the conversation and asked if I hate it when my wife does this or that. I always have one answer that I hold strong to. I tell him how bad my wife would feel if she knew I was at work bad-mouthing her.

I respect her enough to never participate in this type of activity and to always speak highly of her.

SHOULD I GO BACK

11. Talk to her.

My wife and I are just like every other couple. We have our arguments, but we're learning to work them out more efficiently.

When we were dating, and during the first year of our marriage, I did what most guys do. I closed off when we had an argument. This method of problem solving proved to just make the argument worse. It didn't matter what we were arguing about; I would become unresponsive and unable to resolve the matter at hand. I've learned to open up more and talk about it, and it has made a world of difference. Even if I thought I was right and knew her bad day was fueling some of the anger, I've been learning to let things go and open up more.

Most things aren't worth a heated argument and should just be forgotten the moment they arise. If you can't shake it, then talk to her, but don't let it build up. Bottling it up will only end in an explosive argument where hurtful things are said that can't be taken back.

12. Sex? Not without romance.

What do men think about at least once every minute?

What do women think about at least once every minute?

We usually answer with a big grin and say "sex" where she might say "shoes," "shopping," "that new book I want to buy," "my dream vacation," "what my friends are up to," "why the color green is so out dated," "a new purse," "ice cream," etc. This is why when you say, "Wanna have sex?" she often answers with, "Not now!" She's not constantly thinking about it like you, so when you bring it up right after she's been telling you about her day or when she asks, "What do you want to do for dinner?" you'll most likely be rejected.

Try a little romance to get her in the mood, and remember that timing is crucial. I've found that when she's walking out of the bathroom and I say, while standing naked in the hallway, "Hey, wanna have sex?" I will, without a shadow of a doubt, be rejected!

I've also discovered that when she wants to cuddle and kiss me, this doesn't always mean sex. This means she really wants to hold my hand and kiss me. My wife is living in reality, whereas I am often basing my actions off my thoughts.

Try holding her hand and kissing her first. When you do, the outcome might be different. You might actually get that sex you've been thinking about every minute for the last fourteen hours since you woke up.

13. Plan a regular date night.

I like to take my wife out at least once a week. This is our date night, and it lets us feel like girlfriend and boyfriend.

We like to do the standard dinner and a movie, but we also like to branch out and try new things for fun. We've gone indoor rock climbing, and to concerts, and we've even just hung out at home and made something amazing for dinner. The magic doesn't have to die because you're married, but there are things you need to do to make it feel like a date.

I have what I like to call "where do you want to go" syndrome. It's date night, we're about to go out, and I think maybe she won't like the restaurant I've chosen. But in reality, she just wants me to make a good decision and take her out. She doesn't want to have to think about it or do anything but enjoy my company.

14. Take her shopping.

A lot of my friends talk about what a pain it is that their wives want to take them shopping or want them to walk around the mall while she introduces them to all the new clothes she wants to try and fit into your closet because hers is full.

My wife likes me to take her out shopping. When I can tell that she really wants that new pair of shoes or shirt, I'll often break down and buy it for her. We try to manage our funds in a way that we know we can afford little things here and there.

I overheard a guy at work talking about how much he hates going grocery shopping with his wife. He prefers that she do all the shopping because he simply does not like it. I like to go grocery shopping because we're often really busy with school and work. This allows us to spend some time together and plan our meals.

15. Learn to enjoy chick flicks.

I would love nothing more than to come home and see my woman in a Phillies jersey waiting to watch the big game with me that evening or have her tell me she's just been dying to watch the entire Band of Brothers series all day long, and that she has purchased steak for dinner.

This scenario is very unlikely, but as I'm more willing to watch what she wants, she is more willing to watch what I want. I've made an effort to watch movies that interest her because she enjoys them, and as I've done this, she has been just as willing to sit down and watch something I like.

16. Be healthy.

This is something I've struggled with my whole life. I mean, I'm a guy!

Keep in mind that you being healthy will directly affect her. If you struggle with a low self-image, then it's time to grab the bull by the horns and lose weight and eat healthy. There are many resources out there to help you meet your health goals. Find what works for you.

Good health will help you take control of your life and show her that you really care about her and want to be around when you have kids someday.

17. Pay attention to the little things.

She's just come home; what's different? Did she mention a new haircut yesterday, or was she talking about getting promoted at work? I have about thirty seconds to point out the obvious before I hear her say, "So?"

Paying attention to the little things is very important because these are often the things she wants you to notice. This doesn't mean that you have to be constantly jotting down her hair appointment dates, but it does mean you should make a habit of knowing your spouse and being more attentive to the unimportant things. I guarantee most men can tell you where the scratches or nicks are on their car and give exact locations and estimated dates and times of when they happened. Or they'll notice a smudge on the flat-screen TV the moment they sit down watch the baseball game.

So, give some of that same attention to your wife. She's the most important person in your life, and this is a great way to express it. Pay attention!

18. We all need outlets.

I am interested in many things and have many hobbies. I like to try new things and learn new skills because it's important to me. These outlets are healthy for you and for your spouse as they keep you both happy and balanced.

I believe, dropping everything and spending all your time together would cause problems for your marriage. My wife loves working out and collecting Disneyland memorabilia; whereas, I teach martial arts and have a healthy obsession with the Philadelphia Phillies.

Outlets are wonderful as long as they do not interfere with your marriage. Have your outlet and be passionate, but do not let it get in the way of your relationship.

19. Take a vacation together.

We all need to get away from time to time, and a great way to do this is by taking small vacations together.

I worry about providing for my family and making sure we have the funds to live, but I've found it isn't a problem to save a little extra money and spend some of it on a vacation together. A vacation doesn't mean an expensive tropical getaway in Tahiti or a three-month tour of Europe. But it does mean little getaways once in a while.

Spend the money. It's worth it, and you'll both come home feeling rejuvenated and ready to take on life once again.

20. Be her biggest fan.

Most men are very passionate about something. Whether this be a sports team or hobby, you dedicate a lot of your time and thought to it.

Your wife is more important than any sport or hobby, so be her biggest fan. Dedicate yourself more than you would to anything else in your life. Go out of your way to introduce her when you run into that old friend from school. I tend to throw an extra word or two in there when introducing her to people. I'll often say, "This is my beautiful wife."

If your hobbies and interests are receiving more dedication than she is, then there needs to be some self-evaluation.

21. Let her teach you, and don't be defensive.

When your wife asks you to do something like pick up the stuff you've decided to throw everywhere after coming home from work, or tells you your jokes were a bit inappropriate, it's not because she's nitpicking you; it's because she loves you.

Listen to her concerns, and learn from them; she will do the same for you. Our male ego often leaves us defensive, and we turn her simple suggestion into an argument. I am guilty of accusing her of nitpicking me. There are things that need to be let go, but when they are things you know deep down you need to work on and she's simply pointing it out, swallow your pride and work to do better next time. These little improvements will keep both of you happy.

This means that you need to be honest with her if she does something that bothers you instead of bottling it up. She might not realize that you feel a certain way if you don't mention it.

22. The power of touch goes a long way.

The largest organ of the body is the skin. It might be as simple as a pat on the back or a touch on her arm, but these simple gestures communicate emotion and are more powerful than we often realize.

The first thing I do in the morning is scratch her back and give her a hug before I leave for the day. When we see each other again at night, we always greet each other with a big hug and kiss. Hold her hand. This skill, developed while dating, is often lost once you're married. But do it as much and as often as you can. Touch her arm, play with her hair, kiss her cheek. These tiny actions are forgotten sometimes because life is so busy, but they are so powerful.

We go through life avoiding contact with other human beings unless we're crammed into a subway train or in an elevator where we're forced to make contact, but when we're home, we shouldn't neglect this powerful way to show emotion to our spouse.

23. You love dishes; you love cleaning even more!

The media tends to have a huge effect on male and female roles in a marriage. We watch the man come home from work, ask his wife when dinner will be ready, then sit on the couch to watch TV and drink a beer. The wife then comes out with a hot plate of food that she serves to him, and they eat dinner. If we based our lives off media portrayals of how it should be, then we would be in big trouble.

Help her cook dinner, or make it yourself for the two of you sometimes. Don't expect her to make dinner for you every single night. But if she does, you should be doing dishes while she cooks.

Help out around the house, and do your best to keep things clean and tidy. A clean living environment is essential for a happy, healthy marriage, but never expect her to do it all alone just because she is the woman. I often come home from a busy day of work, and I'm mentally drained and tired, but this doesn't stop me from helping around the house or fixing dinner.

24. Friends are important.

Let go of friends that bring you down.

If your friends are the type that expect a lot from their wives and are constantly complaining about them, you may need to find new friends. Putting yourself in this environment and being around people who drain you will only result in you bringing that negative energy into the home.

These types of friendships or acquaintances are poison to a marriage. One of my friends was like this, and I finally let that friendship go.

25. Learn to say, "I'm sorry."

I didn't realize how far it can take a relationship by simply saying, "I'm sorry."

We tend to make mistakes in our relationships often, and failing to say we're sorry and letting go of our pride or male ego is one way to really mess things up. If we want her to see us as the man of the house or treat us as such, we certainly need to be man enough to apologize and say we're sorry when we are in the wrong.

As I've been learning this valuable skill, I've realized that it has improved our relationship immensely, and I know it will continue to prove beneficial as we grow old together and face all that life has to throw our way.

26. She's still your girlfriend.

My wife and I were recently at a dinner for my work when a fellow employee's father was talking to us. I introduced her as my amazing wife, and he said, "You mean your girlfriend?" I said, "No, my wife." He persisted that she was still my girlfriend. This seemed strange at first. But then he said, "She's your wife, but she's still your girlfriend, never forget this!"

We looked at each other, and it all made sense because he was right. She is my girlfriend, and I should never forget this because it will help us to never forget when we first fell in love.

Share everything with your wife, and talk to her like a friend. Discuss your issues and dreams, where you want to go in life, and where you want to take the relationship.

27. Keep your eyes to yourself.

A lot of men believe they were born with an unstoppable habit for staring at other women.

This habit is offensive, especially when you do it right in front of your wife. The best way to stop staring at women, if it is a problem, is to simply not do it.

Just like your wife doesn't appreciate you talking about her behind her back, she especially doesn't like you staring at other women, whether you do it in front of her or when she's not around.

28. Be unpredictable.

This might seem like it goes against a lot of what we've been talking about, but it's a great way to keep the magic alive.

I like to do little things for my wife. One of my favorite things is buying her something small for no reason and taking her out when she isn't expecting a date. It's hard to be unpredictable when you're working and taking care of other responsibilities, but I've found that it can be done on a moment's notice.

When you're at the gas station and go in to pay, grab her favorite drink or treat and bring it out as a small surprise. It doesn't matter what you do, but doing it when she isn't expecting it is the best way to go!

29. Counseling can be a good thing.

Don't be afraid to go to a marriage counselor. If you both feel like you need it at some point, then don't hesitate.

SHOULD I GO BACK

My wife asked me at one time if I would ever go to a marriage counselor if a point came in our marriage where we needed it. At first, I thought about what a waste of time this would be and wondered why we'd ever need to go. But who knows, maybe we'll need to see someone at some point, and I'll need to lose my male ego and realize that things like going to a marriage counselor are sometimes necessary. Because I'm a guy, my pride gets in the way a lot of the time because I think I'm above certain things. But this same pride is the reason we've had some of our arguments.

If we ever decide during our marriage that we need to go to a counselor, then I'll do it and try and learn something from it.

30. Learn to laugh.

Laughter has been such a wonderful part of my marriage.

We spend a lot of our time together laughing. I'm always somewhat glad other people aren't around to see how funny we think we are.

What a fantastic list! Keep in mind that my son-in-law was just twenty-five years old when he wrote this list. Both he and my daughter had already learned a great deal about respect in a marriage, and about how to take care of each other.

That said, they are now thirty-six and thirty-seven and have been married for fourteen years. I definitely think they were onto something that works.

It baffles me when I realize how many of us get married, settle in, and immediately start treating each other as though we are the enemy!! What is that? Why are we so anxious to get married and then start acting like we can't wait to get out?

When my daughter and her husband had been married just two years, they already had eight—yes, eight—sets of friends who were getting divorced. Something needs to change!

It's as though we have forgotten that marriage takes work! When you take two different people from different backgrounds with different experiences and put them together, it's going to take work. It doesn't matter who you are married to; it takes work!

I think the one question we should be asking ourselves before we decide to get married is not, "Is he everything I ever wanted," but rather, "Am I willing to love, honor and cherish my spouse AND work as hard as possible to make this marriage successful?"

CHAPTER ELEVEN

HOW DO I FIND THE RIGHT PERSON TO MARRY IN THE FIRST PLACE?

That is the burning question.

The first, and sometimes the only, thing we consider when we're looking for a potential mate is that head-over-heels feeling we get when that certain guy just does something for us. Do you know what I'm talking about? And, guys, you do it too.

While I'll agree that we'll all know within just a few minutes of meeting someone whether or not we'd like to get to know someone better, it's simply not enough that your heart just skipped a beat. Marriage is a complicated matter that should take more consideration than a lot of us give it.

So, what should we be looking for?

We would probably all agree that experiencing that "Oh Baby" feeling is a must. It's pretty hard to move forward unless you're getting at least a little spark. Where some of us fall short is that we think it means everything. We allow ourselves to look past so many important things because of it. We tell ourselves we're in love, and we're deliriously happy. We just found ourselves in a place where we'd like to stay for the rest of our lives. What we forget to consider when we're in that state is just about everything else.

And what happens when we interpret that spark as love, and wind up saying, "I do" too quickly? Many of us end up years later in a marriage that has some pretty serious problems because we forgot to realize we have major differences going on within the relationship. And it's a little late, after a few years of marriage, to realize this person really isn't the right one for you. By then, you're looking at options that aren't really all that desirable.

Remember, that spark wears a little thin over the years – it changes - and we need to have some solid anchors holding us together at that point.

So how do you get yourself in that place where you can get your heart to settle down and actually think through things logically before deciding to marry someone?

You know what I'm going to say.

Sit down and make a list!

Only you can decide what you are going to want and need in a marriage partner over the long haul. It's important that you get yourself to look at this person from a logical point of view. Some of the things you want are preferences, but some of the things you need are mandatory for a good, solid, long-lasting marriage.

The spark is a great place to start—at least you know you are attracted to this person. But let's move on to the bigger picture.

Ask yourself a few very important questions:

- Is this person genuinely happy?
- Is this person kind and loving?
- Is this person smart about money?
- Does this person have the same values that I have?
- Does this person feel the same way about family that I do?
- Is this person loyal?
- Is this person truthful and genuine?
- Do we have enough in common to have fun together?
- Will this person make a good parent and do we want the same number of kids?
- Is this person mature enough to handle the difficulties of marriage?
- Does this person handle problems in a productive way?
- Is this person concerned with my well-being?

The list you just read involves things that allow us to love a person in a deep and meaningful way over time even when the spark has worn off.

Being infatuated with someone's looks or with the way they dress or with the importance of their job or the amount of money they make will not make us love someone more deeply over time. Having been where I've been, I now know a long and lasting relationship has nothing at all to do with these things.

It wouldn't be a bad idea either to seek the opinions of people who know you best and find out what they see in the person you are considering. Love is blind, but not always in a good way.

Think about the people you've loved for a lifetime—your close friends, your parents, your siblings, etc. Ask yourself why you have loved them your whole life. What is it about them that keeps you connected? Consider looking for some of those same qualities in a spouse.

Now don't start thinking there is a perfect person out there—one who will fulfill all your needs on a daily basis and make all of your dreams come true. Don't be unrealistic in your expectations of a spouse, but look for someone with the qualities you need for a happy marriage in the long run. Look for someone who will love, honor, and respect you, and you will stand a far greater chance of making your marriage work.

Just don't forget, there are two sides to that story of success. You need to be the kind of person who will also love, honor, and respect your spouse.

So, if you're not quite there, start using the tools in this book to improve and instill these qualities within yourself and become the kind of person that another person wants desperately to be with.

CHAPTER TWELVE

CREATE YOUR PERFECT SPOUSE

Let's take the topic from chapter twelve just a bit farther.

Remember when you were a teenager or maybe even just a small child and you created lists of the qualities you wanted to find in your future spouse?

Wouldn't it be fun to get ahold of those lists and see how close we came to getting what we thought we wanted?

For most of us, I think we might find that our lists fell short, and instead, we actually chose to marry someone we fell in love with, rather than someone who met all of the criteria, right? Sure, you most likely found someone with the big, important things from your list, but the tall, dark, and handsome probably fell by the wayside.

My daughter and I were sitting around talking about things one night, and we came up with the following exercise to help us all see some things a little more clearly.

This exercise is fun!

I call it "Create Your Perfect Spouse."

And I want you to do it because it may be a real eye-opener for you; it was for me!

The first thing I want you to do is make a list of all the qualities you want to see in your husband or wife. It's just like that list we were talking about earlier when you were determined to find that perfect person—you simply weren't going to settle, remember?

Now I came up with sixteen things within about five minutes. Let me share them with you just for fun:

- Kind
- Honest
- Good provider
- Strong religious values
- Sense of humor
- Loves kids
- Enjoys family time
- Trustworthy and trusts me
- Happy and secure
- Has integrity
- Interested in health
- Loves dogs
- Likes to travel
- Sensitive and romantic
- Not a tight wad
- Enjoys food and cooking

SHOULD I GO BACK

Now I want you to throw a bookmark in at this point while you make your list so you can spend as much time as you need. And don't open the book again until you're finished.

* * *

You're back! You should have your list written down and be ready to move on.

Now I want you to make a list of which of those qualities you actually see in your husband or wife. They have to come from your list so you can basically check off the qualities he or she has. Now as I did this part of the assignment, there were a couple of things I thought: "He's pretty good at that" or "He has half of that. (He loves food but doesn't cook). But he wants to learn to cook, so he definitely gets points for that." And that is something I could help him with.

Do you see where I'm going with this? Write down the qualities he or she has. And then write down the qualities he or she has the potential for. I want you to do that so you can see that he or she may actually be closer to achieving credit for a quality that you didn't think he or she had at all until you did this assignment.

You might be surprised!

Now, throw in your bookmark again and close the book because I want you to complete this portion before you move on. No reading ahead!

* * *

All right, let's move on to the final portion of this exercise.

Now I want you to make a list of each of the qualities from the list that YOU have. That's right! This is where the real eye-opening part comes in.

Close the book one last time, and come back when you're finished with the list.

* * *

How did this exercise turn out for you?

I'm hoping you are beginning to realize that none of us have every perfect quality. We all fall short. I'm betting if any of my exes made a list of qualities and I looked it over, I'd realize I fell short of their expectations in many ways.

The point is none of us are perfect. And knowing that will hopefully help us accept each other in a more loving and realistic way. I'm hoping we can all begin to focus more on the qualities our spouses have rather than the ones they don't.

It takes effort to do this!

Is it possible to create our perfect spouse in reality? Probably not, but encouraging, helping, motivating, and inspiring each other to achieve potential qualities is a close second. None of us will ever reach perfection, but knowing that we are doing what we can to help each other improve can create an environment where anything is possible.

I think we can expect more from one another.

I think we can set aside the expressions of disappointment when things don't go our way.

I think we can stop the nagging.

I think we can stop the arguing and just let go of the little irritations.

I believe we can challenge our partners in a way that just might help them become someone they never thought they could be.

You just never know where all this could lead; Maybe your marriage will improve.

Get to work on creating your perfect spouse!

CHAPTER THIRTEEN

INDULGE ME, HONEY

Just for fun, I decided to include this chapter. I came up with this idea one day while I was in Florida sitting on the beach.

My friends and I were sitting out on the beach in our beach chairs, sipping Diet Coke, and watching people. I love to watch people at the beach; it's intriguing to see how people are dressed, who they are with, and whether or not they care what people think.

I think you can learn a lot about a couple by watching them in that environment because you know they are on vacation. So where is their attention directed? For instance, are they playing together or holding hands and kissing? Or are they completely absorbed in their own activities? Are they enjoying each other's company and talking to each other? Or is one sleeping while the spouse swims in the ocean?

We watched one couple sitting on opposite ends of a beach chair the entire time we were out there, never talking, never touching. We saw several couples walking along the beach holding hands. But we also noticed one couple walking along, and one was three feet behind the other.

It's always interesting to see how people interact with each other when they are alone together in a vacation spot. You know what I mean?

Anyway, I started to come up with some of the things I would enjoy having my husband do for me or know about me if I ever do take the chance and get married again, one last time.

That got me thinking even more that maybe we sit around wishing our spouses would do certain little things for us, when the reality is, they don't even know those things are important to us or mean anything to us.

I realized we need to be more forthcoming with the things we need from our spouse, instead of getting annoyed when they don't do them even though they have no clue!

So, what do you think about telling your spouse you want some things – things like this:

1. Please laugh at my jokes; I think I'm funny, and I'd like to think you think so too.
2. Please tell me often that I look beautiful.

3. If you're having trouble coming up with a gift idea, go with the JCrew gift card.
4. When you do something thoughtless, bring me my own whole, fresh strawberry pie.
5. When I'm cooking, rather than say, "Do you need help?" just take charge and start helping.
6. Hug me for no reason, expecting nothing in return.
7. Come home early on Friday so I'll think you're excited to start our weekend.
8. If you want to make love but can see I'm hesitant, give me a back rub—works every darn time!
9. Take the initiative to make special dinner plans on occasion and take me to a new place.
10. Hang out with me more often, and just "do nothing" with me.

Too often, we think our husbands or wives should be able to read our minds. We think they should already know that we wanted them to do something for us.

Tell your spouse the things you'd really like from him that would make a difference to you. I kept my wants to ten, but it's your list, so go for it. And then ask your spouse to make you a list in return.

I've left some room below for you and your spouse to start working on your own lists. Don't just throw anything on there; it took me three weeks of thinking about things off and on before I really had a golden list that I would want to turn over to a husband. Give this some real and sincere thought. The goal is to have things on there that will really make a difference to you in your relationship. It has to be personal.

This is her list:

1.
2.
3.
4.
5.
6.
7.
8.
9.
10.

This is his list:

1.
2.
3.
4.
5.
6.
7.
8.
9.
10.

Now, husbands, once your wife gives you the list, work hard to do what's on it and try to make her happy! If you don't, well, don't say I didn't warn you!

And, wives, if you expect your husbands to do these little things for you, then you'd better be willing to do the same for him!

Now take your lists and put them somewhere—in your desk drawer, on your bathroom mirror, on your nightstand, someplace you will see them on a regular basis. Refer to these lists often so you can remember to do things on occasion that will light his or her fire. Pretty soon, you'll be doing these things in your sleep and looking for new things to add.

CHAPTER FOURTEEN

TEN REASONS TO KEEP IT TOGETHER

Often, when we get to that point of thinking we want a divorce, all we can focus on is why we want out. It becomes really hard to logically think through all the reasons why we should stay together. And it's nearly impossible to look into the future and see how our decisions are going to affect life in the long term.

I want to leave you with my list of "Ten Reasons to Keep it Together" before I end on "Should I Go Back." And then I want you to add to this list to make it personal to you.

Before you make your final decision, I'd like you to really delve into the ten items below, take each one individually, and try to look into the future for yourself and for your family.

You are faced with an important, life-changing decision. Don't rush into it without considering every detail of what it will mean down the road.

1. You once loved each other enough to get married.

It's amazing that we can go from being so excited to get married we can't think straight, to wanting nothing more than to just be done with our marriage. How does that happen? Tell yourself it's worth a shot to try getting back to that place where you really loved each other. We all know mature love sets in after about two years. We can't stay blissfully and blindly in love forever, but we can choose to love each other as mature grown-ups for the rest of our lives. And I believe mature love trumps those early stages of love if we can get to that point of solid commitment and security. That is what true love is meant to be.

2. After the war of divorce dies down, you will actually miss your spouse to some degree and the life you had—believe it or not!

Once you've had some time to get used to being single again, and even years later, when you're involved in another relationship, you'll ask yourself, "Why didn't I try this?" or "Why didn't we do that?" because you'll see things from a whole different perspective. You'll realize that your new relationship has many of the same challenges, plus a few you never thought of. It becomes much easier to see the good that existed once you're out of the situation. The trick is to try and see it when you're in the heat of the battle.

3. There is most likely a lot of good in your marriage; you just need to remember to focus on the positive.

It doesn't matter who you're married to; there is some good in almost every person and in almost every marriage. If there weren't, you wouldn't have married your spouse in the first place. Once the bad starts outweighing the good, we have a problem. And I believe it's pretty easy to let that happen if we're not putting in the effort. That said, it does take two, and if your spouse is not willing, divorce is most likely inevitable.

4. You will always long for your original family to be intact.

If you haven't lived this, it's probably hard to understand. But I know from experience that this will happen. If you ever get to where I am, with a few divorces under your belt, you'll see that the idea of being married to the husband you had your kids with, assuming it wasn't something terrible that led to the divorce, might seem like a dream. Don't give up on your marriage until you know for certain you are willing to live with the craziness, the sadness, the loneliness, the chaos, the anger, the resentment, the regret, and all the other emotions that can pop up at times after divorce.

5. Starting over is no picnic in the long run.

The initial excitement of having a new life, maybe a new house and a new husband will eventually settle down, and you'll be back to having to make that same decision you were faced with before—to choose whether or not you are going to love your spouse unconditionally. Are you married to someone this time that you will choose to love, or will it be easy to leave when the going gets rough?

6. No one will ever love your kids the way you and their other parent do.

Yes – there are exceptions to this rule. I personally know people who love and trust their stepparent as much or more, in some cases, than their biological parent. But a person being handed the role of stepparent has an enormous job to do. And most of us don't really know how it's going to work for us until we're right smack in the middle of it! The truth of the matter is, it's not always easy to love someone else's children. This one's for the kids: no one is really ever going to replace their dad or their mom.

7. Keep it together for the future grandkids.

I don't have grandkids yet, but I know it won't be long. And I can't help but think it would be so nice to be an intact, original family.

There are some wonderful people who are pretty good at being step grandpas and grandmas, but you will likely experience complications at times. You may want to spend more time with your grandkids and help out with them and be around them. But will your spouse want that as much as you do? The grandkids will experience a little bit of what the kids experienced—being bounced around between grandparents and step grandparents. It's definitely something to think about.

8. You've built a lot of memories; keep building.

I've started over with memories three times. The problem is, most new husbands don't like it when you have pictures or memories of your family before him. I've had to get rid of reminders of the past a couple of times, and that doesn't really seem fair. I made sure my kids got pictures and scrapbooks of their father, but it's just another complicated thing you may have to deal with when you get divorced.

9. The big picture is what's important when it comes to family.

Sometimes we get so caught up in the thought of getting away from a spouse that we forget about all the other members of the family and extended family. We can sometimes complicate a lot of people's lives and destroy relationships. If we can begin to focus our efforts on the big picture—the family as a whole—maybe it will become easier to resolve conflicts and save families whether there is a divorce or not.

Keep it together to keep life from becoming more complicated than it has to be.

Your life and everything in it will simply become more stressful, more difficult, and more complicated after divorce. There is almost no way around it. I don't care who you marry. I don't care if you stay single. Your life will become more complicated—issues with the kids, money, relationships with the ex-family, emotional baggage, the logistics of being a single parent, time constraints, the list goes on and on and on and on!

I was listening to Dr. Phil one day, and he made the statement that "we in this country get divorced too easily." He said you have to earn your way out of a marriage by exhausting every avenue of rehabilitation before getting a divorce.

In the end, he said, there should be no unfinished emotional business.

Once again, let me say that I have learned during my journey that it doesn't matter who you are married to; it takes work! The problems and issues may come in a different form, but they will still come. And you are going to have to work through those too.

SHOULD I GO BACK

You have so much to offer as an individual and as a partner in a marriage. Work to become your best self, work to be the person others want to be around, and work to be the kind of spouse your husband or wife deserves. If we can all do that, the world will be a much happier, healthier place.

CHAPTER FIFTEEN

SHOULD I GO BACK

Going back to the beginning and that burning question –

Let's talk about going back to your marriage to give it one last shot.

Is it a good idea?

Is it worth another try?

Should you do it?

I do think, in some instances, it's a good idea. And here's why. Sometimes people get stuck in a place where they can't seem to move forward. Some couples do genuinely wonder if they might be able to start over and make a go of it this time. Sometimes there are unresolved emotions that need to be dealt with. The point being – there can be any number of reasons why couples can't quite pull the trigger on divorce. And yet, they remain in a place of limbo.

And that's why, based on my own experience, I believe going back in for just one more try could actually help you move on. Just to remind you about my story – as betrayed as I felt, as hurtful as my husband had been, and as devastated as I was at the thought of another divorce – I still wanted to see if I could avoid this one and stay married. I wanted to see if maybe I could forgive and forget. I wanted the hurt to disappear, and I wanted to just forget about everything that had happened and start fresh. I think it's a normal reaction and one that most divorcing couples experience at some point in the process.

I went in for one last try.

You already read about my experience and how hopeful I was. There was a time when I sincerely believed that maybe – just maybe - we could actually put the past behind us and move forward and enjoy a rewarding and successful marriage. If we could get through this and hold it together, really wanting each other, this would be the greatest achievement of my life!

But here's what I learned.

People only change if they want to change.

People can change temporarily, but it takes a major amount of effort, a huge amount of self-awareness, and a sincere desire to make lasting changes for a person to change for good. And we're usually talking about major things, not little changes that are easy to make.

Once a person has been forgiven, they can quickly forget about the pain they have caused.

People think they want to change.

Sometimes people will be motivated to change for you at the thought of losing you.

But ultimately – most people resort back to the behaviors that are comfortable for them.

My husband stood to lose a great deal - a wife who faithfully loved him, his entire extended family who gave him the benefit of the doubt and accepted him with open arms, a step daughter who adored him and who he loved like his own, 3 dogs, an adventurous lifestyle that we created together, lots of great friends, and many, many things that would have been devasting for most people to lose.

And yet, he simply could not and would not change his behavior.

In my case, going back was the blessing in disguise. Going back is what made me realize I did not want what my husband had to offer. But I had to know it in my heart and soul. The experiences I had during those last few months completely shut down my feelings for him and my desire to make our marriage work. I knew then that I had to move on. But more importantly, I WANTED to move on.

If you find yourself in similar circumstances where you believe you need to divorce but can't quite pull the trigger – maybe it's time to consider going back, whether that's literally (after a separation), or figuratively (maybe you've been living in separate bedrooms or just simply shut down from each other).

Maybe your marriage will be the success story. And if so, I wish the very best for you from the bottom of my heart. I have seen a few couples make it work after taking a step back, realizing they really do want to be married to each other, and both people going back in 100 percent. One of those couples is a close family member. They have been back together for about three years, and I pray every day for them that they will be able to keep their level of commitment high enough to make their marriage last a lifetime.

Relationships are hard.

Two people who are ALL IN and completely committed to each other is what it takes to make them succeed. And if you don't have that – you're going to have to decide if staying in the marriage is really going to be worth it to you in the end.

CHAPTER SIXTEEN

THE ENDING TO MY STORY – AT LEAST FOR NOW

I have been single now for several years. Just over eight at this point. I'm happy that I have been able to do this - for several reasons. Not the least being the fact that I needed time to recover. My kids needed to recover. We all needed me to get my life built back up – without the help from anyone other than myself.

I left that last marriage with almost nothing. My ex took the houses he owned beforehand, of course; But he also took the house we owned together. As women often do, we find other things more important like our peace of mind, our surroundings, stability for our children. I took the "deal" because it was more important to me that my daughter stay in our home until high school graduation than it was for me to get a settlement at the end.

For me, this arrangement more than worked out. I have recovered over the past eight years in a very big way. I have worked extremely hard, and I also have the Lord on my side. Without my Savior, I have no idea where I would be at this point. These things have been very apparent over the years, and I am grateful.

Going back to my second marriage for a bit, I want to write about this because I think it can help many of you. When I married my second husband, I was thirty-two years old. He was Forty-four, and he had three teenage daughters. I had two younger children. Our life was chaotic for many reasons. But the main point I want to make is that while I was married, I struggled with his ex-wife and his daughters. I would not allow myself to love them. I was angry because I was left with the burden of dealing with the drama, and I did not like it. Their mom had re-married and left the State, and all I could see was how this was affecting ME. I kept pushing back and created so many issues. In the end, I just couldn't handle this life. Once I was out of that marriage and began to realize how poorly I handled my relationships with these people, I realized just how much hurt I had caused. I contributed to the chaos instead of stepping back and trying to realize that we were all in this marriage together. How much better it could have been for everyone involved if I could have accepted the situation and helped these individuals have a better life.

Hindsight.

Fast forward nearly thirty years. Those daughters are sisters to my youngest who was born during that marriage. That bond has brought us all together in a special way. It started when my daughter would go to family gatherings and asked me to come with her. Friendships started to build with each of those daughters. And then their mother and I started to become friends. She and I decided to schedule lunch and we have since spent time talking through everything that happened back then and working through the negative feelings we all had.

This has been a true blessing in my life. We are family because of my daughter. She is the glue that binds us all together, and we like that fact. My second husband passed away about a year ago, and a lot of healing has taken place since that time between us all.

Life holds a lot of surprises. Divorce doesn't need to be the end of the world. For those who can work out their differences and remain in a loving marriage, I admire you. For those who realize they must leave, I feel your pain. And I know you will be alright. In the end, all we have are our relationships. Having as many of those intact as possible is a wonderful goal to work toward. And sometimes, the people we battle with wind up being some of our deepest friendships in the end. I remember hearing an admired leader say, "If we don't like someone, it's because we don't know them yet." I love this quote and I think of it often.

My third divorce held the most pain for me because I had such a huge investment in that marriage and our life was so good.

But honestly, I wouldn't trade anything that I've experienced. My life during the marriage was good, and my life after the divorce has been wonderful. I have learned so much, and I have endured a lot. I have become a strong, independent woman who can thrive on her own. I don't need to be married, but I'd like to be if I can find someone who can match my energy and contribute to my life in a positive way. If I can find someone that I feel myself wanting to give my love to, I will marry one last time. If not, I know I'm going to be just fine. And it took a lot for me to reach this point.

Just as with my stepdaughters in my second marriage, I have kept a relationship with my stepson from this third marriage. He is wonderful, and we have stayed in close contact. He knows not to talk about his dad to me and that does not come into play at all in our relationship. I don't feel bitterness towards his dad – I just feel adamantly that he does not deserve to be in my life anymore. Period.

When I received that very first phone call on August 30, 2012 (it's hard to forget the date), I broke into tears. I knew at that moment that no matter what happened, my life was about to change. And it did.

New job, new home, new experiences, new friends. But also, old friends who have been there for me the entire time, family who were and continue to be my biggest support, kids who have loved me through it all. Life has been good. Life has been better than it ever has for me. I have enjoyed this time I've taken for myself.

I love where I am at this time in my life. And I look forward to the new adventures that await.

The things I have gained from three marriages and three divorces were not what I would have chosen, but they have been invaluable in contributing to the way my life has gone. I have gained confidence in who I am, I have gained four step children whom I love, I have gained a friend in another ex-wife. I have gained a relationship with my first ex-husband's wife and daughter. I have gained the ability to be strong and take care of myself. And I have gained a greater empathy for those who struggle in marriage.

What would I do differently if I had a do-over? What would any of us do? It's always easy to know after the fact what you should have done, but none of us have that luxury. We all do the best we can, and I believe we have the experiences in this life that each of us personally need so that we can become the people we are meant to be. This belief has made me less judgmental over time of what other people are going through.

We all do dumb things. We all make mistakes. But we have to start looking at the bigger picture. Never look back with regret. Always look back and ask yourself, "What did I learn from this?"

If you do find yourself in a situation of having to divorce and start over, let me assure you -- you can get through it, and you will be fine. You will find capabilities in yourself that you did not realize you had.

See this as a new adventure, a new chapter in your life.

Keep a positive outlook and start considering the ways that you can create a new life for yourself. Sometimes we find ourselves in places we did not intend. When that happens, run with it and look for the opportunities that lie within.

Adults can handle these types of changes to their life. But keep your focus on the kids. Help your children see that even though their parents may be divorced, they will do everything in their power to at least remain friends and keep a good family dynamic -- no matter what. Kids want to know they can have access to both of their parents any time they want. I believe that's the greatest gift you can give to your children. They will feel secure and they will not have to worry about making either parent upset.

When you do remarry, if you can do it - let your new husband and his family hold on to as many of the elements from their life before you as much as possible. They need to be able to keep familiar things close so they can be happy and have a healthy outlook. It's not easy. But it can be done.

Try to love them and adopt the mantra "the more the merrier."

People need love. We all go through difficult experiences and the more we can support and help each other, the happier we all will be. I know how difficult it can be to bring families together and try to create a loving environment. Not everyone is going to be all in. But others will be. When my first husband remarried, his new wife was wonderful to me and to my kids. We created a safe environment for the kids, albeit, not perfect. But there was a lot less stress to deal with because of her attitude. And her attitude made my attitude better.

I wish you all the very best in your life decisions. Don't let guilt or judgment, depression or frustration creep into your decisions. No one knows better than you what is best for you and your own family. Don't let others' opinions weigh you down and don't let anyone tell you whether you should stay married or get divorced.

Do what you need to do and be happy!

CHAPTER SEVENTEEN

A FEW FINAL WORDS
– FROM A FRIEND

Just yesterday I was sitting with a close girlfriend of mine at lunch. As we were talking about someone she knows who has recently gone back into the dating pool, she asked about my book and insisted that I get it written and published. She didn't know I was almost finished writing it.

I want to leave you with some of her words of wisdom. She and I have been through very similar experiences – that's one of the reasons we're such close friends. The other reasons are because we like a lot of the same things – a couple of those being golf and cookies.

As we were talking over our salads, she said some pretty powerful things that I think are important for you to know and understand from the perspective of a mother who spent a good portion of her child rearing years single. She, like I, divorced when her children were very young. She thought they would never know the difference and they'd be just fine – after all, children are resilient, or so says the world. But she has since concluded that kids are not all that resilient. We both believed all along that our children were doing just great. My girlfriend told me that she and her husband made all of the arrangements for their separation before telling their kids – her husband had his new apartment all set up with rooms and beds for each of them. They had everything in place and thought the transition would be a piece of cake. And it was – for mom and dad. They gathered the kids together one night and told them "we're still your parents, we love you, and you'll be able to spend as much time as you want with both of us - your lives won't be that different!"

If you came from a family where your parents remained married – imagine back to the time when you were a child, growing up in the secure surroundings of your family. And then try to imagine how it might have felt to have your parents gather you around the dinner table one night for a meeting to tell you they were splitting up, and your dad was no longer going to live with you. Can you imagine what that would have done, not only to your heart, but to your entire world?

Both my friend and I are strong. We knew how to take care of ourselves and our children. But for a child, that is simply not enough. Life is just more difficult when you try to do it on your own without the support of a loving spouse, especially when you have young children.

When we find ourselves wanting a divorce (different from actually needing a divorce) we don't necessarily give that much thought to how the kids are going to be affected. Just like my friend believed they were doing just fine all along.

But then they grew into adults, and that resilience started to look a little more like rebellion. Our kids were hurt by their parents, and there is just no getting around that fact. No matter how hard we try to make everything alright, our kids are going to experience trauma and all of the fallout that comes along with it. Each kid will suffer in their own way – some worse than others, but suffer they will.

My friend and I agreed that looking back now, it would have been a whole lot easier to work through the problems of our first marriages than it has been to take on new marriages.

These are hard facts. And if you're considering divorce I just want you to fully understand what lies ahead. Be prepared and be ready for some difficult challenges that you absolutely will face – whether they come while you are raising your children or later in life.

I talked with another friend this week who left her husband out of necessity four years ago. Her story is difficult too, but she said it's some of those big moments in life where you really feel the impact. For example, she had a daughter graduate from high school recently and another daughter graduate from college – both on the same day in different parts of the country. She managed to attend one ceremony and then hop a plane and attend the second ceremony all in one day – all alone. She said I spent the entire day missing my original family.

I know how she feels. There have been many times when I have grieved the loss of, not necessarily my husband, but that original, intact family unit. I have a lot of people in my life who love me and support me, but there is a hole that I believe can never be completely filled after a divorce – especially if it happens while you are still raising your kids.

Just some food for thought.

Thank you for reading this book and allowing me to share my personal experiences with you. Each of yours will be different – some things will be similar, but I hope there was something here that helped you in some way – even if it just a little bit.

Take care of yourself. Take care of your kids. Find the joy you are looking for in your life and keep loving and growing and being happy.

With Love!
Janeen

ACKNOWLEDGMENTS

I find myself where I am today because of the many wonderful people who have loved and supported me throughout my life. Without them, I honestly don't know where I would be.

Dirk, you are my only son and the child who came into my life first. You changed everything for me when I became a mother, and I will always cherish the day you were born. You had the inexperienced young mom who made lots of mistakes, but never forget that I love you. You have so much to give. Take care of your sweet Amber and always let her know how special she is.

Tia, the first time I held you in my arms, I knew you were special. That has proven to be true, and I am privileged to have you as my daughter. You have become a beautiful, confident, wonderful young woman. I am proud of you, and I love you. You and Jake are blessed to have each other.

Gabby, you are my sweet baby. You came along when I was older, and you like to tease me about that. But the truth is, I'm a much better person and mother now than I was then. You are reaping the benefits of much experience. You are beautiful, talented, and funny. I am in awe of what you have accomplished in your twenty-three years, and I love you with all my heart.

Mom and Dad, you are both in Heaven now, and I miss you so much. Without you, I don't know where I would be. You supported me through all my trials and remained the lasting influence on my children. They are who they are largely because of you. I am blessed to have had you as my parents. I will always love and appreciate you for everything you have done for me and my family.

Susan, Ruth, Karyn and Julie, you are my closest and dearest friends. You are the ones who have helped me keep my sanity throughout all of my sadness, stress, and hard times. You are examples of strength to me, and without you, my life would be a lot less fun, that's for sure.

Amy, Julie, Karen, Stacie and Tina, you came into my life in the most wonderful way. I was guided to move into the house in your neighborhood when I married my third husband. Heavenly Father knew I would need you all when my marriage ended. Your friendships have truly saved me.

Thank you to all my friends whose examples I have used in this book. So many of us have lived through difficult times, but we love and support one another because we know what it's like to feel alone. Hang in there, all of you, and keep moving forward in a positive direction.

To many of my colleagues and coworkers throughout the years who have influenced and inspired me, each of my jobs has been a joy because of you people whom I've come to know and respect.

To my neighbors and friends, you are wonderful. I am blessed to live near and associate with people of your caliber. You make life joyful and adventurous.

And finally, to all of you who are working to make your marriages better, remember the things that are important, remember to work hard, and remember that you have the power to change. You also have the power to create a new life for yourself if you find that it becomes necessary. I promise you will find joy no matter what you chose to do.

ABOUT THE AUTHOR

Janeen began her career in Broadcast News in 1995 after graduating from Brigham Young University. She was immediately hired by KUTV 2News in Salt Lake City as a Reporter/Anchor, where she stayed until her third child was born in 2000. After going back to work briefly, Janeen decided this time, she wanted to enjoy every minute of every day with her beautiful daughter. So, she left 2News and began her freelance career.

She has worked on many commercials, corporate videos, and branded spots over the years. She also acts as a Spokesperson for many companies. But divorce would eventually bring her back into the workplace. She accepted an offer at ABC4 where she switched gears and worked as an Account Executive and part-time on-air talent for seven years – which she loved.

But with a better offer on the table, she decided to leave her job at ABC4, and she went back to KUTV

2News – this time as a Marketing Consultant at the beginning of 2023. Janeen likes to consider herself somewhat of a freelance marketing consultant, as she is also involved with a company called Fuze Technologies that uses a patented green technology to permanently kill bacteria and eliminate odors on fabrics and surfaces.

Janeen loves beaches, road trips, fitness and dogs -- she had three little ones until one by one, they all went home to heaven. She would love to someday get another dog or two when her schedule slows down a bit, but admits to being the world's worst dog trainer - and so she waits…

She is a divorced mother of three – her two oldest, a son and a daughter, are married and have successful careers. Her youngest, a daughter, is just about to graduate from college, with plans to go on to law school. On the verge of becoming a true empty nester, Janeen is working hard for a bit longer so she can play once in a while, travel, and enjoy her grandkids – if she ever gets any.

Printed in the USA
CPSIA information can be obtained
at www.ICGtesting.com
LVHW042151180524
780663LV00001B/71